Transforming The Enterprise Through COOPERATION®

Transforming The Enterprise Through COOPERATION®
An Object-Oriented Solution

Dan Shafer
David A. Taylor

With significant technical assistance from
Lawrence Rozier

PRENTICE HALL, *Englewood Cliffs, NJ 07632*

Library of Congress Cataloging-In-Publication Data

```
Shafer, Dan.
    Transforming the enterprise through COOPERATION : an object
-oriented solution / Dan Shafer, David Taylor.
    p.   cm.
    Includes index.
    ISBN 0-13-088451-0
    1. Cooperation (Computer file)  2. Business--Computer programs.
3. Object-oriented programming (Computer science)   I. Taylor, David
A.,        . II. Title.
HF5548.4.C652S5  1993
650'.0285'5369--dc20                                      92-30378
                                                              CIP
```

Publisher: Alan Apt
Production Editor: Mona Pompili
Art Director: Cheryl Leaphart
Graphic Designer: Ann Dolin
Cover Designer: Eddie Albert

Illustrator: Dan Schumaker
Screen Editor/Indexer: Patter Cross
Prepress Buyer: Linda Behrens
Manufacturing Buyer: Dave Dickey
Editorial Assistant: Shirley McGuire

© 1993 NCR Corporation
Published by Prentice-Hall, Inc.
A Simon & Schuster Company
Englewood Cliffs, New Jersey 07632

The author and publisher of this book have used their best efforts in preparing this book. These efforts include the development, research, and testing of the theories and programs to determine their effectiveness. The author and publisher make no warranty of any kind, expressed or implied, with regard to these programs or the documentation contained in this book. The author and publisher shall not be liable in any event for incidential or consequential damages in connection with, or arising out of, the furnishing, performance, or use of these programs.

All rights reserved. No part of this book may be reproduced, in any form or by any means, without permission in writing from the publisher.
Printed in the United States of America

10 9 8 7 6 5 4 3 2 1

ISBN 0-13-088451-0

Prentice-Hall International (UK) Limited, *London*
Prentice-Hall of Australia Pty. Limited, *Sydney*
Prentice-Hall Canada Inc., *Toronto*
Prentice-Hall Hispanoamericana, S.A., *Mexico*
Prentice-Hall of India Private Limited, *New Delhi*
Prentice-Hall of Japan, Inc., *Tokyo*
Simon & Schuster Asia Pte. Ltd., *Singapore*
Editora Prentice-Hall do Brasil, Ltda., *Rio de Janeiro*

Trademarks

NCR is the name and mark of NCR Corporation.

COOPERATION® is a registered trademark of NCR Corporation.

BIM is a derivative of Channel Computing, Inc.'s FOREST & TREES software program. FOREST & TREES is a trademark of Channel computing, Inc.

Document Conversion incorporates technology under license from Mastersoft, Inc. Mastersoft is a trademark of Mastersoft, Inc.

IBM® is a registered trademark of International Business Machines Corporation.

Information Storage Manager incorporates technology under license from Saros Corpoartion. Mezzanine is a trademark of Saros Corporation.

NewWave® is a registered trademark of Hewlett-Packard Co.

Microsoft®, Microsoft Windows™, MS-DOS®, Excel® and OS/2® are registered trademarks of Microsoft Corporation.

ORACLE® is a registered trademark of Oracle Corporation.

Remote Application Access is based on DynaComm®, a registered trademark of Future Soft Engineering, Inc.

SQLBase®, SQLHost® and SQLNetwork® are registered trademarks of Gupta Technologies, Inc.

UNIX® is a registered trademark of AT&T Bell Laboratories.

Acknowledgments

Without the able technical assistance and insatiable curiosity of Lawrence Rozier, this book would not have been as complete or as much fun. He is in a real sense a co-author of this work and his name on the title page testifies to the debt we acknowledge owing him.

Michael J. Komichak wrote an incisive and insightful manual entitled *Doing Business with COOPERATION,* which we found quite useful during our study and understanding of COOPERATION and how it could be used in a business enterprise.

John Casserly of NCR was patient and supportive throughout the process of shepherding this book from an idea to a finished manuscript.

Finally, our respective families were, as usual, not only supportive but even uplifting and encouraging. It is difficult to overemphasize their contribution to this and all our other work.

Contents

Introduction ix

Prologue: The Advantages of Object Technology xi

Part One: USING COOPERATION

1. The Power of COOPERATION 3
2. The COOPERATION Environment 9
3. The COOPERATION Desktop 27
4. Scripting the COOPERATION Desktop 39

Part Two: MAXIMIZING COOPERATION

5. Getting Started with COOPERATION 53
6. The Application Environment 61
7. COOPERATION Services 77
8. Strategies for Deployment 91

Epilogue: Transforming the Modern Enterprise 113

Index 125

Introduction

NCR's new COOPERATION system is the first full-scale enterprise computing system based on object technology. This distinction caught the attention of both authors early in the development of the product because we are both ardent advocates of object technology and its application to enterprise management. Our shared interest led to further explorations of COOPERATION and our subsequent collaboration on this book.

In working with pre-release versions of COOPERATION, we have found that it reflects both the power of object technology and the difficulty of scaling this or any other technology up to the enterprise level. Although COOPERATION doesn't solve all the problems of enterprise computing, it does a remarkable job of elevating the advantages of objects to the corporate level and combining a vast array of computational resources into a unified environment. And it's clear from our experience with successive versions of COOPERATION that NCR is intent on refining this product as rapidly as possible to provide additional functionality and tighter integration.

This book provides a brief overview of what COOPERATION is and how it can be used to help manage an organization. We intend it to serve both as an introduction to the product for those who are considering its adoption and as a guide to companies who are already putting the system to use. For the latter audience, we must emphasize that the book does not replace or duplicate the extensive documentation that comes with the COOPERATION product. Rather, it provides easy access to the product, allowing end users to get started quickly and to locate additional information in the documentation as they require it.

We expect this book to be read by people with a wide range of backgrounds, including executives, managers, end-users and implementers. The organization of the chapters reflects the needs of these diverse audiences.

The Prologue offers a brief summary of object technology and its advantages over conventional approaches to building software systems. We encourage all readers to at least review this chapter. For those who are new to object technology, it will provide an easy introduction to the basic concepts behind this technology and help them understand the chapters that follow. For those who are already familiar with object technology, the chapter will provide a quick calibration to ensure that the messages we send in the rest of the book invoke the appropriate mental methods.

Part One of the book, Using COOPERATION, is written for the person who will use COOPERATION but will have little or no involvement in managing the system. In this section we summarize the overall capabilities of the product, then introduce the use of those capabilities from the perspective of someone who simply wants to get her work done more effectively.

Although COOPERATION is a complex system, it presents a simple and consistent interface to users. Anyone familiar with the current generation of graphical user interfaces can begin doing productive work with COOPERATION after reading no more than the first three chapters.

The fourth chapter, which deals with scripting office activities, is a transitional chapter. It introduces a simple method by which end users can begin to customize their COOPERATION desktops, automating routine tasks and freeing their time for more productive activities. This chapter can be read immediately after Chapters 1 through 3, or it can be postponed until after the user has become familiar with the COOPERATION environment.

Part Two, Maximizing COOPERATION, is written for the people who will be involved in the installation and management of a COOPERATION system. End users are invited to browse this section if only to get a glimpse of takes what place behind the scenes. But the material is necessarily more technical in nature and assumes more familiarity with computer hardware and software.

Part Two can be read by itself but we don't encourage it. Even those with a deep knowledge of the underlying technology will benefit from seeing COOPERATION from the user's point of view before they begin to design their installation of the system.

Although Part One may suffice to allow an end user to get started with COOPERATION without studying its documentation, Part Two definitely does not confer the same benefit. Everyone involved in the management of a COOPERATION installation must become familiar with the full suite of documentation that accompanies the product, and each will need to read selected documents in detail. However, Part Two of this book should make this documentation more accessible and ease the transition. It also provides some tips and techniques for getting the most benefit from COOPERATION that won't be found in any of the manuals.

The book closes with an Epilogue on the future of enterprise computing. We believe that object technology will forever change the way organizations function, allowing them to act far more coherently and intelligently than ever before. In the Epilogue, we explore some of the ways in which COOPERATION may contribute to the emergence of this new kind of organization.

We would like to express our appreciation to NCR for supporting the creation of this book. We would also like to applaud the people of NCR for having the vision to see the essential role that object technology will play in the future of corporate computing, and for having the corporate conviction to act on that vision.

We are pleased to contribute, if only in a small way, to the dawn of a new age of enterprise management.

PROLOGUE

The Advantages of Object Technology

COOPERATION is based largely on object technology. In fact, it is easily the largest, most ambitious commercial application of this technology to date.

Why did NCR use object technology instead of more conventional programming techniques? It is unlikely that COOPERATION could ever have been brought to market without the use of object technology. A short excursion into the inner workings of this technology will help explain why it was essential to building COOPERATION and, more important, why it is essential to constructing any enterprise management system.

In this chapter, we will look first at the basic principles of object technology. Then we will examine how these principles are applied within COOPERATION.

INTRODUCTION TO OBJECT TECHNOLOGY

Object technology is one of the most important technological ideas in the history of software. It has become commonplace to claim at least some degree of object orientation for software even if that claim is marginal at best and patently false at worst.

The details of object technology are well beyond the scope of this book. Indeed, dozens of titles—some by the authors of the present work—have been published on the subject and more appear daily. But a basic understanding of the fundamental principles of object technology and of their advantages is important enough to occupy us for a few moments.

We will begin this discussion by comparing software objects to manufacturing hardware components. We will then talk about how and why to create reusable objects. The notions of combining procedures and data as well as creating classes and objects will be covered as well. Finally, we will describe the idea of composite objects before we conclude by discussing briefly how message passing works among objects and why messages support a better model for business software solutions than the traditional procedural approaches.

SOFTWARE BY ASSEMBLY

Most explanations of object technology tend to launch immediately into the wonders of dynamic binding, the power of polymorphism, and the problems of paradigm shifts. While these are all essential aspects of the technology, plunging directly into such deep conceptual waters leaves most readers gasping for air and wondering why the technology is so hard to understand.

The truth is that object technology is really a simple and intuitive approach to building software. The object-oriented approach essentially consists of constructing programs out of prefabricated parts known as *objects*. Each of these software objects corresponds to a real-world object or event such as a product, purchase or payment. As you can readily imagine, assembling software out of existing components is considerably more efficient than programming each new application from scratch.

Figure P-1: Programming by Assembly

In fact, the advent of object technology is often compared to the Industrial Revolution that took place in manufacturing 200 years ago. Prior to the Industrial Revolution, all goods were crafted by hand, with each component created from scratch to fit its niche in a particular, individual product. The great innovation of the Industrial Revolution was to standardize components and manufacture them in quantity, allowing products to be created by assembling these components in an efficient, standardized sequence.

The benefits of this new approach were overwhelming: Products could be assembled far faster and much less expensively, and the quality of the resulting output was more consistent and easier to control. There was considerable resistance from craftsmen and their guilds to the radical concepts of modern manufacturing, but the benefits made their adoption inevitable and manufacturing was forever transformed.

Despite that fact that software development is often called "engineering," the actual process of software construction has been far more of a craft than most developers would care to admit. With the advent of object technology, we are making the same transition in software that was made 200 years ago in manufacturing. By assembling programs out of standard object components, we can construct these programs far faster and much less expensively. Moreover, because new programs consist primarily of existing, proven components, the quality of these programs can be greatly increased.

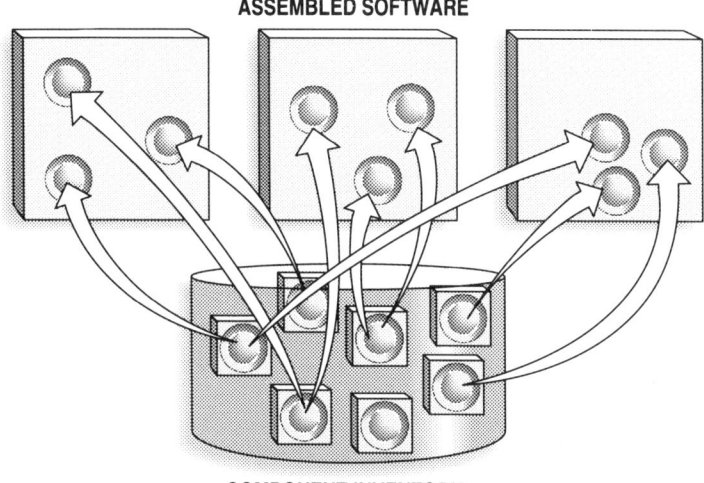

Figure P-2: Working with Reusable Components

That, then, is the essence of object technology: A transformation of software development from a craft to a standardized fabrication process. This transition is bringing major benefits to both the producers and the consumers of software. Although the object approach has met with some resistance from developers who have long been accustomed to crafting programs, we believe that, as with the Industrial Revolution, the benefits of software by assembly virtually assure its universal adoption. It is to NCR's credit that they understood the coming transition years ago and made the decision to take full advantage of object technology in COOPERATION.

CREATING REUSABLE OBJECTS

As with manufacturing, programs built out of objects may require many components that are all constructed in a similar way but differ in their actual details. Thousands of bolts are required to assemble a car. These bolts may vary in their size and pitch, but they all perform the same function and are manufactured in a similar manner. Similarly, in the case of a purchasing system, there are thousands of purchase orders that take on the same form but differ in their actual details.

In manufacturing, each kind of part is typically fabricated on a dedicated factory line. In object technology, there is also the equivalent of a factory line. It is called a *class*, and its function is to produce objects of a particular form. Each specific object that a class produces is known as an *instance* of that class. Like bolts off a production line, each instance can vary in its details but all instances of a class perform the same function and are created according to the same generic template.

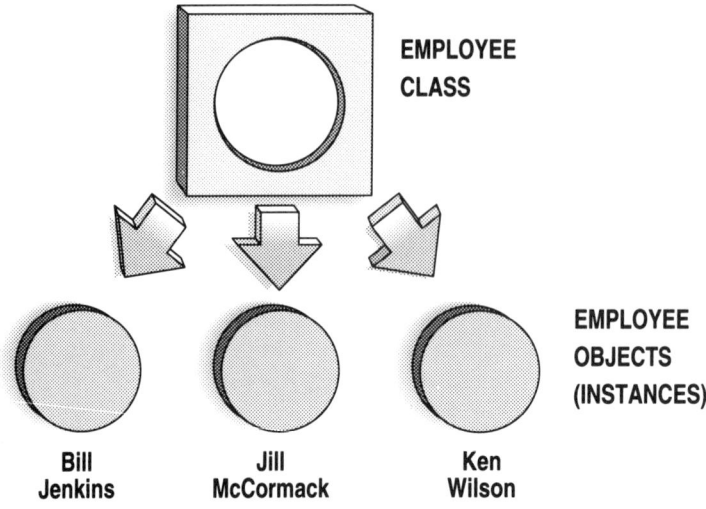

Figure P-3: And Employee class Creating Instances

For example, in an object-oriented information system, employees are represented by objects. The way this actually takes place is that a class is defined that reflects the overall characteristics of an employee. To represent any specific employee, the class is asked to produce a new instance of the class. This new employee instance—which is also often spoken of as an employee *object*—has all the same characteristics (name, department, job title, and so forth) as all other employee objects. But the new instance differs from other instances of the employee class in that it has a different name, belongs to a particular department, and so on. As new people are hired, new employee objects are created. As people leave the company, the objects that represent them are removed from the system and either destroyed or stored away for archival purposes.

The basic requirement for assembling programs out of objects, then, is a good set of reusable classes. In general, the more classes you have on hand, the faster you can assemble new software because most of what you need is already at hand. Similarly, the better the quality of the classes you use, the higher the quality of the resulting software. Building up a good library of high-quality, reusable classes is essential to gaining the maximum leverage from object technology. Over time, this may represent a substantial investment on the part of an organization. However, the investment will repay itself many times over because every component stored in the class library is coded only once, not recreated for every program.

By the way, here is a area in which the analogy with manufacturing breaks down, but in the best possible way. Unlike an inventory of hardware components, which has to be constantly replenished from suppliers, the inventory of classes you build up is never depleted. Once you have created a class, you can generate an infinite number of objects from that class with no production costs whatever! In this sense, a class is much more like a complete factory (albeit a specialized one) than a component.

COMBINING PROCEDURES AND DATA

One of the unique aspects of objects is that they combine related procedures and data. This allows each object to fully reflect the behavior and state of the real-world object to which it corresponds. The employee object, for example, would have procedures—called *methods* in the jargon of object technology—that would handle routine tasks such as assigning the employee to a different department or changing the employee's job title. Similarly, the object would contain places to store data—called *variables* in keeping with current programming practice—that retain information about the current department and job title.

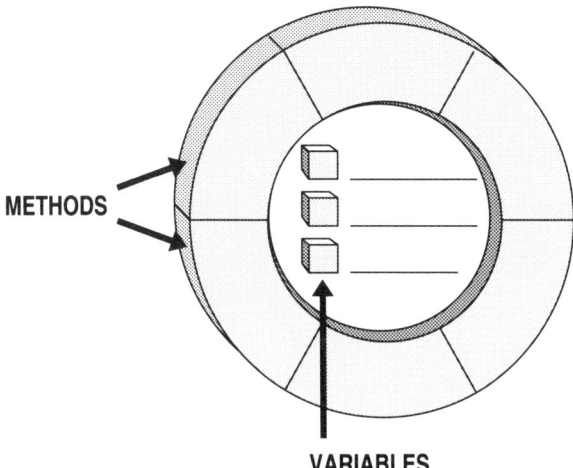

Figure P-4: The Methods and Variables of an Object

This intimate bonding of procedures and data is called *encapsulation*. Learning to use encapsulation to advantage can be difficult for developers schooled in traditional techniques because they have been taught to carefully separate procedures and data. Procedures, they have learned, are relatively stable and are usually bound up in relatively static programs. Data, on the other hand, can change constantly, and is stored temporarily in variables during program execution, then placed in a database for more permanent storage. With objects, both the methods and the procedures are subject to change, and both are maintained in databases when they are not in active use by a program.

The fact that related procedures and data are bound together in a single object makes it much easier to understand and maintain object-oriented software. For example, if you change your procedures for assigning and storing employee ID numbers, you can make all the necessary changes inside of a single object. No other aspect of your information system need even know that a change has taken place.

The internal structure of an object reveals further advantages of object technology. As a rule, all access to variables is by way of methods. For example, if you want to know the total compensation package of an employee, you send the appropriate message to the object that represents that employee. The method invoked by that message will do whatever is required to return the correct value. If total compensation is stored in a variable, the method will simply retrieve and return the value of that variable. On the other hand, if total compensation requires a computation, such as adding salary plus bonus plus the current value of the benefits package, then the method would look up the component values, compute the result, and return the total.

Notice only the employee object knows exactly how total compen-

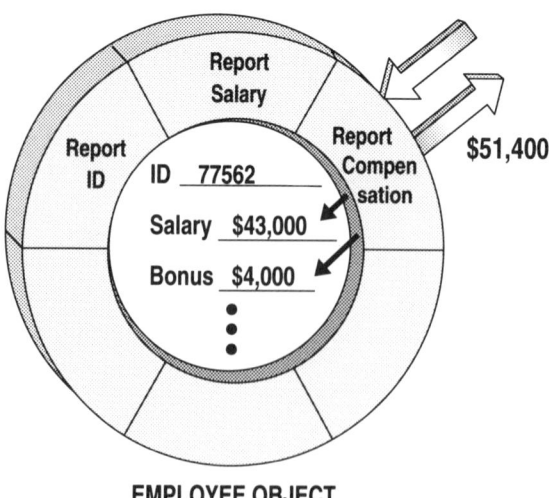

EMPLOYEE OBJECT

Figure P-5: The Internals of an Employee Object

sation is determined. This technique is called *information hiding*, and it confers a couple of important benefits:

- First, it simplifies the system as a whole because no other object has to contain any code to calculate total compensation, nor does it have to know where this information is stored and what type of variable contains it. In fact, other objects don't even have to know whether compensation is a calculated result or a stored value—all they have to know is how to ask for the amount.

- Second, it makes the system much easier to change. You can easily modify the algorithm by which you determine total compensation, or even switch from a calculation to a stored variable. All you do is modify the single object involved. All other objects continue to interact with the employee object just as they always have. In fact, you can make significant changes in the way you value compensation without creating so much as ripple in any of the other objects that depend on this valuation process.

CLASSES, SUBCLASSES, AND HIERARCHIES

Much of the power of object technology comes from the fact that classes can be defined as special cases of each other, *inheriting* all the methods and variables of the more general classes. These special cases, or *subclasses*, can be broken down further into more specific subclasses, creating a hierarchy of specialization that can be nested to any number of levels.

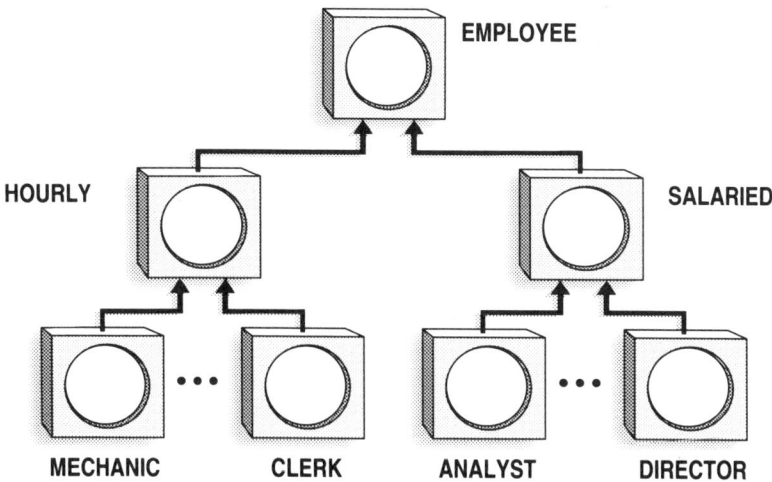

Figure P-6: Part of An Employee Class Hierarchy

The inheritance of methods and variables works all the way up the hierarchy, so that the lowest class in the hierarchy can make use of the methods and variables of the class at the very top.

The use of inheritance has several significant advantages:

- It further reduces redundancy in defining procedures and variables. Each method and variable is defined only once, at the most general level to which it applies. All subordinate classes automatically make use of this definition.

- It is easy to change general-purpose methods and variables. As soon as you change them in any class, these changes are automatically "broadcast" to all the appropriate subclasses.

- The entire concept of defining objects in terms of a hierarchy is a natural reflection of how we think. Two of the most fundamental aspects of human cognition are generalization and discrimination. In object terms, generalization consists of discovering higher-level classes that capture common characteristics, and discrimination is breaking classes down into subclasses to reflect important special cases.

BUILDING OBJECTS OUT OF OBJECTS

The variables contained in objects can contain simple values such as dates, numbers and dollar amounts, or they can be contain references to other objects. This latter alternative greatly increases the power of objects to represent complex, real-world objects. In effect, you can build objects out of objects, and these component objects can contain other objects, and so on, down to any level of detail you like.

For example, an employee object would almost certainly contain the person's home address. You could easily define that address as a series of variables, including street and number, city, state, and zip code. But employees aren't the only objects that will contain addresses—customers, vendors, government agencies, service providers, and many other kinds of objects also contain addresses. Instead of duplicating all the address fields for each class of object, it's much easier just to define an address object and use that object to contain the address.

Of course, this means you have another class to define. But there's no extra work involved since you have to define all the variables and methods for handling addresses in any case. The advantages of separating these out into a separate class are:

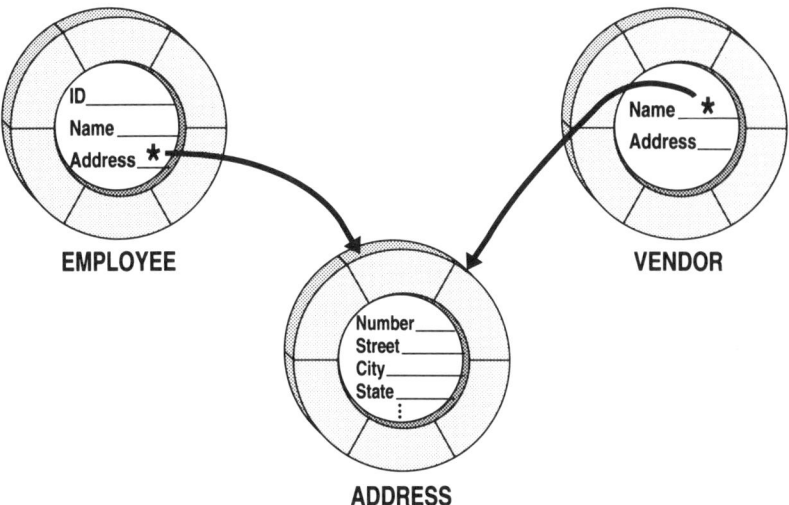
Figure P-7: Two Objects That Contain Addresses

- You only have to do the coding for addresses once. The new address class becomes another object factory that will do your coding for you every time you need to work with addresses in other objects.

- You ensure that addresses are handled identically throughout the company. If different departments have special needs for addresses, these can be handled through subclasses. But the generic code for addresses should be universal.

- It is easy to make changes in the way you handle addresses. The classic example is switching over to 9-digit zip codes. By isolating zip codes to a single class, you only have to make the change once, not in every class that contains an address.

THE POWER OF COMPOSITE OBJECTS

Objects that contain other objects are called *composite* objects. The advantages of composite objects go well beyond the efficiency advantages described in the case of addresses. The real power of composite objects is that they allow you to build high-level, interactive software elements that correspond naturally to the complex entities in your business. Instead of having to think in terms of fields, tables and computations, you can think in terms of everyday business objects. In effect, object technology allows the computer to come up to your natural level of thinking rather than forcing you to think in terms of bits and bytes.

Consider a personnel evaluation form as an example. This form would be represented by an object that might contain a variety of other objects, including an employee object, a series of rankings and a narrative summary. The employee object, as we know, would contain other objects such as address objects. The rankings would probably be contained in what is known as a *collection* object, which is a special kind of composite object that can contain a variable number of objects of the same type. Using a collection to hold the rankings isn't strictly necessary, but it's a good idea because it allows you to vary the number of criteria on which you rank various employees without having to change the evaluation object.

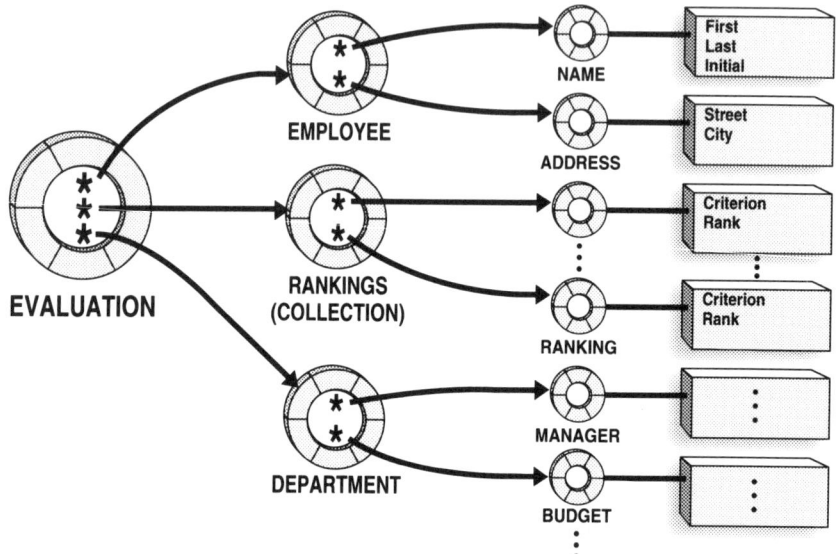

Figure P-8: Components of an Evaluation Object

Drilling down one more level, each ranking contained in the collection would itself be a separate object. A ranking object might consist of a criterion, such as "Work habits," together with a number reflecting the ranking. The ranking object would also contain methods for collecting and displaying this information. For example, instead of displaying the ranking as a number, it might display a series of checkboxes and place a check mark in the corresponding box. This would make the evaluation form easier to fill out and review, but would require minimal storage space because only a single digit would be stored in the object.

COOPERATION uses composite objects at every possible level to allow you to think about your business terms rather than computer terms. For example, all you would do is click on an icon to bring up an evaluation form, select the employee from the list of people that report to you, fill in the rankings by clicking in the appropriate boxes, and typing in any narrative text you want to add by way of a summary.

COOPERATION also uses a variation on the concept of composite objects called *container objects*. These are high-level objects that contain other high-level objects, providing still more power to organize information and activities into meaningful groups. For example, you would probably group all the information about a given employee into a container object called a *folder*. This folder might contain an electronic copy of the employee's offer letter, an image of the employee's photo ID, the accumulated evaluations that you and previous managers have given this employee, and other related material. For convenience, you would probably group all of your employee folders into a larger folder called "Staff."

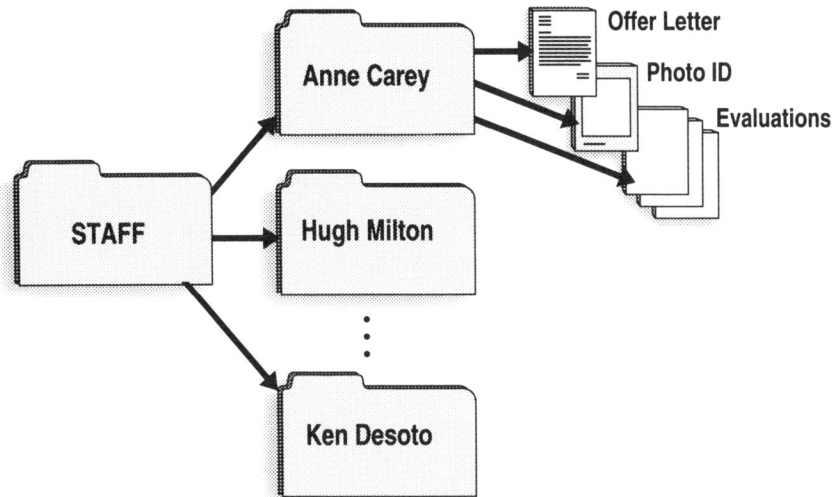

Figure P-9: Organizing Information with Folders

Container objects not only package information conveniently, they make it easy to store, exchange, and share information. For example, you could use electronic mail to send an entire employee folder to a new manager if the employee transfers and all of the associated information would go with the folder. Alternatively, depending on corporate policy, you could declare any or all parts of an employee folder available to that particular employee but not to other employees. Ordinarily, the employee would be allowed to read the folder at will but not to have the ability to change its contents. How-ever, again depending on policy, the employee might be assigned the right to insert self-evaluations into the folder prior to the formal evaluation date, or to place a response to your evaluation in the folder after the evaluation had taken place.

INTERACTING THROUGH MESSAGES

It should be clear by now that with the basic mechanisms of classes and objects we can build systems of any complexity we desire. There is just one minor flaw—these systems couldn't actually *do* anything. There is no way for one object to get another object to carry out its methods.

Here's where a third and final mechanism comes into play—that of *messages*. A message is simply a request by one object asking another object to carry out one of its methods. All interactions between objects take place by way of messages. They are the universal medium of object communications.

A message consists of three parts: the identity of *receiver* object, the name of the method the receiver is being asked to carry out, and any additional information, or *parameters*, necessary to perform the requested method. For example, a message might look like this:

Morton_Stein increase_salary_by $3500

The receiver is *Morton_Stein*, an employee object. The method to be carried out is *increase_salary_by* which, as the name implies, modifies the *salary* variable, and the single parameter is *$3500*, the amount of the increase.

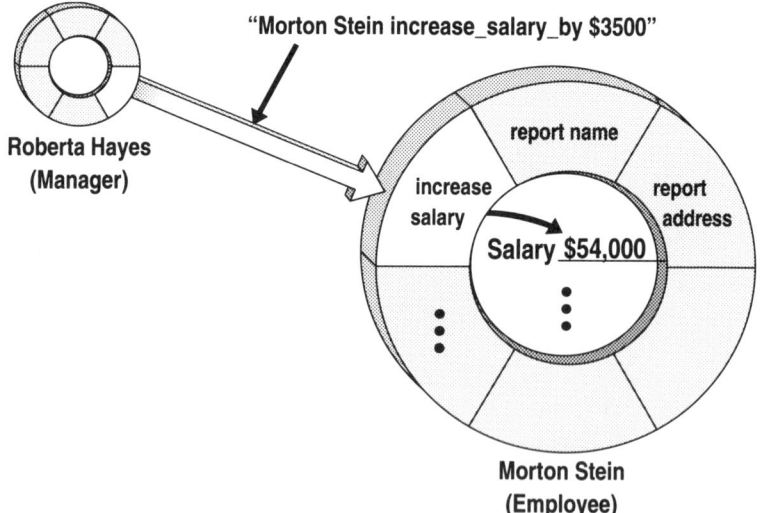

Figure P-10: A Message to an Employee Object

Messages are the basic means through which objects interact in COOPERATION, but they are not the only means. Above the layer of messages, COOPERATION provides *agent tasks* and other scripting tools for automating the behavior of objects and their interactions. For example, it is possible to choreograph the entire employee evaluation cycle, moving folders from desk to desk and obtaining the required entries and signatures, by using COOPERATION'S high-level scripting language to automate the dispatch of messages that cause objects to carry out their functions. Each step in such a task generally involves message traffic among objects.

A NEW PERSPECTIVE ON SOFTWARE

It is interesting to see how this new approach to software design and creation converges with and supports the modern-day need to model business enterprises, a subject to which we devote considerable attention in Chapter 8.

All businesses consist of a range of functions and objects, controls and relationships. Some of these elements are high-level and abstract, such as corporate mission statements, personnel policies, and the like. Other elements are quite low-level and detailed, such as the exact sequence by which a manager is to fill out a personnel evaluation form. Between these two extremes lie a number of other levels of complexity and abstraction of data and procedures.

Before the advent of object technology, business modeling processes generally had to make significant trade-off decisions between high and low levels of abstraction and detail. What often resulted was a half-way solution to the modelling problem: too much abstraction to be useful to day-to-day staff who had to implement policies, and too much detail for the policy makers to be able to see the long-term effects of policy and strategy change.

This trade-off, and its attendant often-unsatisfactory results in terms of the business model, can be traced directly to the isolation of data and procedures from one another. The information needed to make a decision was often a detail while the procedure for obtaining it was inaccessibly abstract.

When object technology came along, it enabled business modelers to bring to the desktop the high-level controls such as COOPERATION's Business Information Monitor that enable policymakers to observe and model mid-range and long-term effects of decisions. It also enabled them to hide all of the gory details of how these monitors and other objects work and interrelate by encapsulating them. The result, as you will see through the rest of this book, is a level of business modeling ability that has been impractical without special-purpose tools.

HOW COOPERATION LEVERAGES OBJECTS

COOPERATION takes full advantage of object technology not only in the way it supports and facilitates the business modeling process described in

Chapter 8 but also in the way it handles virtually all routine tasks of the enterprise.

At the highest levels of the COOPERATION solution, object technology enables the implementation of frameworks which form the basis for much of the rest of the COOPERATION architecture.

The Object Management Facility (OMF) is another example of how COOPERATION leverages its object technology base to give users more power and involvement in the enterprise and its operations without requiring them to understand details of the system. Ultimately, every program running on a workstation, every object stored on the workstation's local disk, must interact with the OMF on the server. This interface is hidden from the user, who is unaware in COOPERATION even of the *existence*, let alone the storage location, of files, or applications. The user interacts with documents and lifelike objects.

At the COOPERATION Desktop, the user gets a very strong sense of the object orientation of the system. The Desktop, which is the focus of Chapter 3, is organized both graphically and structurally around the notion of objects. For example, users don't have to open an application, choose a document to work with, open that document, and then issue a "Print" command. Instead, they simply find the document's object, represented as an icon on the Desktop or in one of the folders on the Desktop, and drag it to the Printer Tool object. That simple act results in all of the processing required to print the document being handled for the user.

In fact, it is even misleading to talk about files in the world of COOPERATION. They are there, but their existence is all but transparent. In the discussion of how printing works in COOPERATION, for example, to be strictly accurate, we would have described the user as finding a specific object such as "Joe's Evaluation Form" and dragging its icon to the Printer Tool object's icon. The object actually encapsulates both the document and the application that operates on that document.

One of the places COOPERATION's object technology is most apparent to the user is in the use of compound documents. A compound document in COOPERATION can contain numerous kinds of objects: formatted text, plain-text notes, graphics, charts, and, eventually, even full-motion video and voice annotations. Each of these elements in a compound document object is itself an object.

Compound documents are, in fact, just one of the many types of objects COOPERATION users create and work with. Other examples include:

- folders, which contain documents and other objects
- database queries
- Business Information Manager icons and packages

- desktop agents, which encapsulate scripts that are messages to and between other COOPERATION objects and which can be used to automate and orchestrate even very complex tasks

In short, virtually everything in COOPERATION is an object. This statement oversimplifies some aspects of the design, but it is safe to say that users—both end users and system administrators—will seldom if ever have to think in terms of any element of the COOPERATION environment that is not an object or cannot at least be treated as if it were.

Transforming The Enterprise Through COOPERATION®

PART ONE:
Using
COOPERATION®

1
The Power of COOPERATION

The world has changed so much in recent years that the very observation that it is changing has become a cliché. Changes have taken place in virtually every fiber of the fabric of the world in which we live. Business, far from being immune to these changes, has been buffeted about by the winds and currents of change.

To keep pace with this rapid rate of change, modern business enterprises have turned increasingly to personal computers. This alliance has not always been as successful or productive as everyone involved would have liked. But it has represented—and continues to represent—the best technology available to assist business managers in their quest for efficiency and effectiveness.

This book describes and explains a recent attempt to bring a greater dimension of power, flexibility, control, and effectiveness to this important marriage of technology and business. This new attempt is NCR's COOPERATION, the first enterprise-wide, fully integrated business solution built virtually entirely on object-oriented technology.

THE NATURE OF THE PROBLEM

One of the authors has previously identified four basic types of change that are problems for modern organizations (see Taylor, *Object-Oriented Information Systems: Planning and Implementation*, John Wiley & Sons, 1992):

- globalization
- decentralization
- customization
- acceleration

COOPERATION can help the modern enterprise cope with all four of these classes of change. As the operations of the business disperse geographically and functionally at an ever-increasing rate, and as product customization becomes a necessity due in large part to the diversity of the marketplaces, tools like COOPERATION will become crucial to the success of a competitive enterprise of the 1990's and beyond.

All four of these categories of change seem to call for two conflicting changes in the nature of the computer systems applied to their management. On the one hand, there is a need for *modularity*. Far-flung enterprises with decentralized management structures will clearly be poorly served by monolithic centralized computers and software. On the other hand, the business itself has become so diverse that there is a need for new software solutions to manage increased *complexity*. How can we create small, manageable, flexible modules of software that nonetheless support and facilitate the management of complexity?

The answer, as was demonstrated in detail in the Prologue, lies in object technology. COOPERATION is built fully on the object model and as this book unfolds, you will see repeated examples and explanations of why this technology makes it possible, arguably for the first time, to bring the necessary modularity and complexity to bear on these business problems.

Another part of the answer to the problem of coping with these changes lies in moving the programming marker closer to the actual user of the software being developed. COOPERATION, by the incorporation of several scripting environments, enables even relatively untrained end users to develop mini-applications that solve highly specific and individual problems. This alleviates the burden on an overloaded professional software staff while ensuring that rapid change can be maintained. (We discuss scripting in Chapter 4.)

UNDERSTANDING WHAT'S IN COOPERATION

COOPERATION is a large system. Explaining its component parts and how they work together would require a significant number of volumes. In fact, COOPERATION comes with a substantial documentation set. Our purpose in this book is not to provide you with anything like the level of detail it will take to manage and interact with COOPERATION in your enterprise. It is to give you a clear sense of the essence of the tool and to enable you to understand how COOPERATION's contents can help you manage your enterprise in the current unsettled business climate.

However, a substantial part of our attention is focused on the various components that comprise COOPERATION. The three major components of COOPERATION are shown in Figure 1-1.

The COOPERATION Desktop—the point at which users and system administrators interact with the system and communicate with the rest of the organization—uses an office metaphor to give users a high comfort level with the tools. On the Desktop, users find such objects as folders, In and Out Trays, printers, waste baskets, and documents.

In fact, one of the most interesting and powerful aspects of the COOPERATION design is the ability of users to have access to multiple desktops. They can create and manage a separate desktop for each role they play in the organization: manager, member of a task force, project leader, subordinate, personnel manager, and so forth.

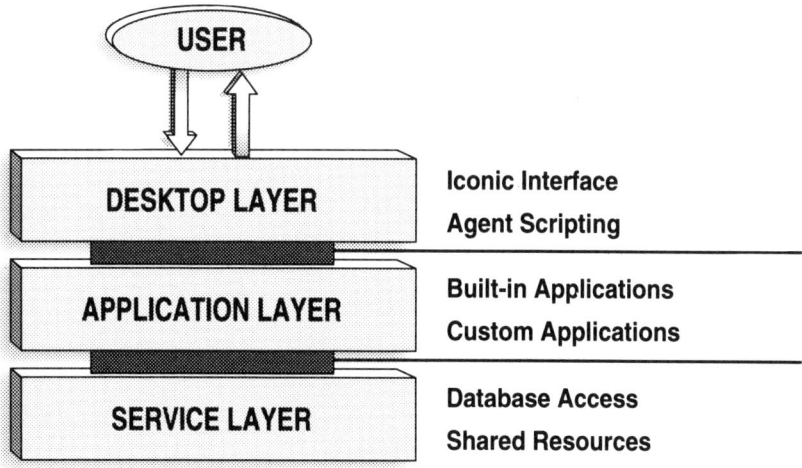

Figure 1-1: Key Components of COOPERATION

Desktop objects and the objects they contain can be given intelligence through the facility of agents. COOPERATION includes a powerful Agent Task Language (ATL) in which even very complex tasks can be automated. Users with no interest in programming or scripting can take advantage of this facility by recording task scripts simply by instructing an object to watch the user carry out some repetitive, multi-step task and then storing the script for that task for later recall. Other users will want to learn and use the ATL to develop individual solutions to specific problems that lend themselves to this approach.

The Desktop and its associated objects are the focus of Chapter 3, while Chapter 4 is devoted entirely to the ATL and desktop scripting.

Beyond the Desktop—although accessed through the Desktop's interface and tools—are two other layers of the COOPERATION environment: the application layer and the services layer. These are, respectively, the subjects of Chapters 6 and 7.

COOPERATION incorporates a number of applications in its object environment. These applications include:

- calendars for groups and individuals
- shared workgroup editing of compound documents
- a tool to enable users to monitor business information
- electronic mail and other communications packages

This application layer also includes facilities for integrating existing DOS software and document files into the new COOPERATION world.

Bridge-building routines and even an interface between the agent facility and these traditional applications are provided.

In the services layer, COOPERATION provides a number of facilities that transcend workstation and application boundaries, including:

- transparent database access
- efficient, effective, and largely transparent document storage and retrieval
- a supply cabinet in which applications can be stored for check-in and check-out by users as needed
- printing services

DESIGNING WITH AND DEPLOYING COOPERATION

Since the emergence of object technology in the 1970's and its initial exploration by a number of companies, users have learned a number of important lessons. Chief among these lessons is the observation that it takes more than a technology to create business solutions.

What is called for is a new set of tools and approaches. COOPERATION supplies a number of good tools. We present in Chapter 8 a new approach, in the form of a seven-step methodology, that enables you to take advantage of the tools to create real-world business solutions. These seven steps are shown in Figure 1-2. Briefly, these steps are:

1. Choose an appropriate business area.
2. Analyze the department's business activity and quantify it.
3. Design the business model for the department.
4. Assign roles to individuals in the department for design and testing purposes.
5. Construct the user and inter-object interfaces to provide a test bed and a design scheme.
6. Execute the design.
7. Deploy the system and monitor its success, modifying iteratively as required.

As you may be able to tell from this brief methodology statement, we advocate a highly iterative and prototype-based approach to system design and deployment. This approach seems to fit naturally with object techniques and technologies, though it is not impossible to use traditional, top-down, structured approaches as well where they are more appropriate.

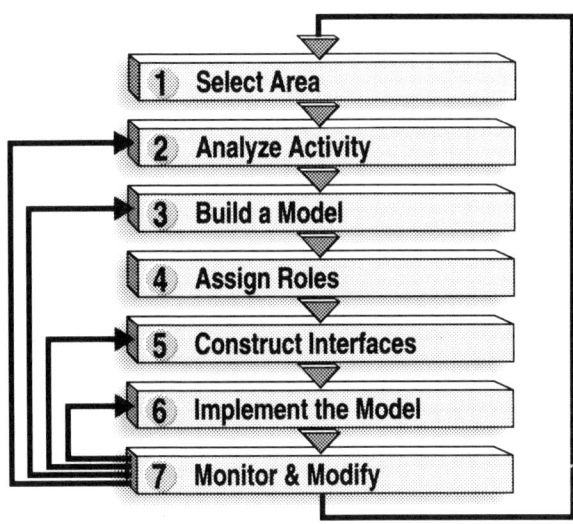

Figure 1-2: A Seven Step Methodology

Once you have one or two departments running efficiently and carrying out their tasks effectively, it is time to begin rolling out COOPERATION through the rest of your enterprise. The process for doing this is also discussed in Chapter 8.

2
The COOPERATION Environment

This chapter provides a top-level look at COOPERATION. After a discussion of the goals of the COOPERATION environment's design, this chapter outlines the major activities supported by COOPERATION. It then provides an overview of the major components available in COOPERATION to accomplish those activities.

This chapter then takes a look at the key elements of the COOPERATION desktop, its application environment, and its services layer. Security of data is important to you. It is also an important aspect of COOPERATION's design, as this chapter will show.

Finally, this chapter discusses the many ways in which COOPERATION is a truly open system from which you can grow and expand without concern for obsolescence.

THE GOALS OF COOPERATION

NCR had dozens of design goals in mind when it began building COOPERATION. Six of these goals became the driving force behind the product. These six design objectives are summarized in Figure 2-1.

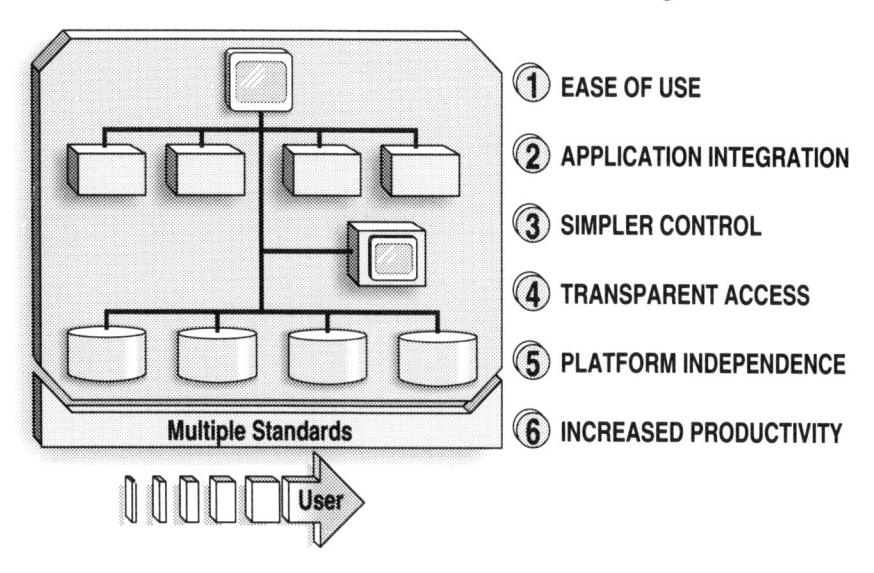

Figure 2-1: Design Objectives of COOPERATION

EASE OF USE

With an intuitive graphical user interface (GUI), COOPERATION makes both learning and using applications easier. The GUI is common from application to application. Once users have learned how to run one program, they have a substantial part of the knowledge they need to learn to use any other application.

In addition to the ease of learning new applications this common GUI provides, COOPERATION users also benefit by being shielded from the complexities of the inner workings of the system. The result is increased efficiency. Numerous studies have detected productivity increases of 58% or more over command-line, text-oriented user interfaces.

INTEGRATION OF WIDE RANGE OF APPLICATIONS

As we have seen, COOPERATION is itself an extensive collection of applications. But it is not a complete set of business applications. This is because established businesses have invested significant amounts of time and money in their existing business software and the data generated and maintained by those applications. These existing systems are often used in mission-critical ways.

As a result of these realities, the design team behind COOPERATION set out to enable businesses to use existing applications in addition to providing a means of integration of new software as work groups adopt new technologies, as illustrated in Figure 2-2.

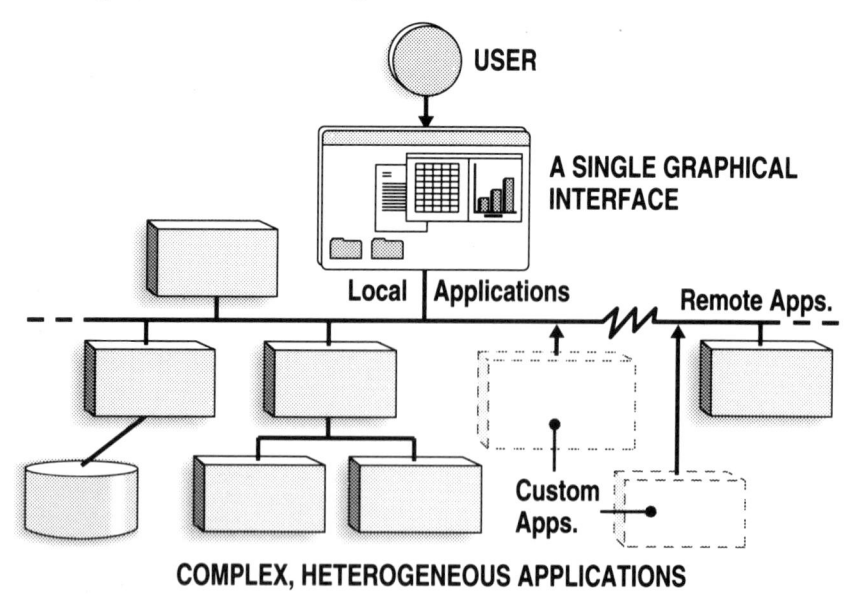

Figure 2-2: Integrating Applications

One clear benefit of this design goal, and its achievement in COOPERATION, is that technology choices no longer need to be tied to or driven by a single vendor. COOPERATION is designed to accommodate software solutions from a wide range of vendors.

SIMPLER CONTROL

It's no secret that computer networks can require substantial amounts of administrative support. System management cost is one of the biggest concerns among businesses that are considering expanding their computer capabilities.

COOPERATION addresses this issue two ways. First, it provides tools that hide management complexity in the system and that support automation of routine tasks. Second, it permits the user to participate in the system administration process wherever it makes sense to do so. For example, as we will see later in this chapter, users can play an important role in maintaining security of the data for which they are responsible.

TRANSPARENT INFORMATION ACCESS

The information that is critical to the operation of the modern business enterprise typically resides in many different places. See Figure 2-3. Managing that information is difficult, even for technically trained personnel. Traditionally, it has been all but impossible for non-technical managers to retrieve and manipulate the information they needed to manage their work groups.

COOPERATION provides for seamless connectivity among systems provided by multiple vendors. This connectivity is transparent to the user

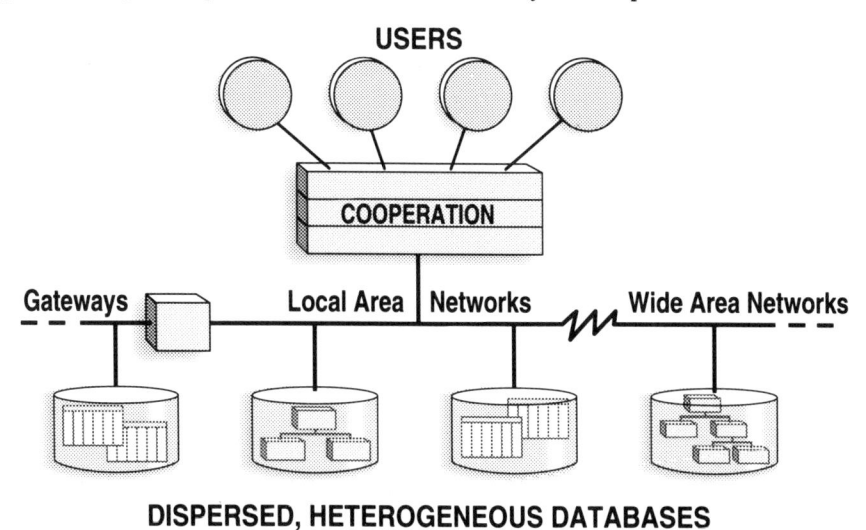

Figure 2-3: Transparent Access to Information

and accessible at the work group or department level through scripting and other techniques. The result is easier access to information, with the related benefit that managers make better-informed decisions and make those decisions more quickly.

PLATFORM INDEPENDENCE

During the past few years, the microcomputer industry has been characterized by much discussion about and confusion over standards. Users want standards. Manufacturers agree, but they disagree among themselves over whose design should form the basis for the new standard. The result is captured in a common remark among technologists: "The nice thing about standards is that you can have so many of them."

COOPERATION hides the differences between processor architectures and operating systems behind a uniform software environment embodied in its GUI. Behind the scenes, COOPERATION supports DOS, OS/2 and UNIX operating systems. Figure 2-4 demonstrates the degree of platform independence COOPERATION will provide. (The initial release, which is the one we worked from in preparing this book, is limited to the DOS/Windows client and OS/2 server platforms.)

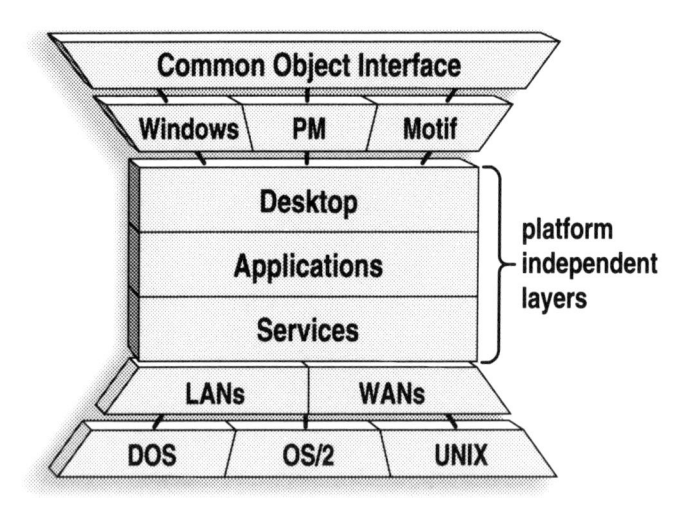

Figure 2-4: Platform Independence

Notice that the platform-independent layers of COOPERATION are surrounded by interfaces at the user level and by operating systems and network communications environments on the hardware level. This architecture makes it possible for COOPERATION to run on multiple operating systems and multiple GUI's without adjustment by the user.

INCREASED PRODUCTIVITY

The first five objectives are technical objectives. All of them are designed to serve the ultimate goal of increasing productivity. By presenting data to users in as timely and easy a manner as possible, COOPERATION increases those users' productivity. For one thing, users spend less time trying to figure out how to get the information they need to make decisions and more time making decisions. They also spend less time waiting, either for a programming team to write some special code to retrieve information they need or for a complex process of data retrieval to be executed.

Another way COOPERATION increases user productivity is by including tools like Desktop Agents and Business Information Monitors that help users automate much of the routine work they must undertake, leaving them more time to focus on crucial decisions that must be based on the information those tasks retrieve.

ACTIVITIES SUPPORTED

COOPERATION includes software to support a wide range of activities. These activities can be divided into those typically engaged in by the end user, those generally in the purview of the system administrator, and those needed by application developers.

END-USER ACTIVITIES

Among the end-user activities supported by COOPERATION are the following:

- electronic mail
- writing, recording and using agents
- compound document editing
- calendaring
- business information monitoring
- data storage and management

A number of other activities that concern the end user are also supported by COOPERATION, but they are largely transparent to the user. These include such functions as:

- automatic document conversion
- access to data stored on the desktop, the work group server, and remote mainframes

SYSTEM ADMINISTRATOR ACTIVITIES

To support the design goal of simpler control over the network aspects of the system, COOPERATION includes tools to enable the work group system administrator to handle tasks such as:

- controlling access to workstations and files
- managing the check-in, check-out, and distribution of licensed software
- diagnosing problems with the system
- backing up critical data
- integrating legacy data and applications

By encapsulating these activities in a common set of dialog boxes, COOPERATION also masks the complexity of these tasks from the system administrator who has to perform them.

DEVELOPER ACTIVITIES

COOPERATION's development environment is built around a related group of object-oriented frameworks. A framework is a library containing code designed to support the COOPERATION environment. As an application programming interface (API), this set of frameworks frees the developer to concentrate on the functionality of a specific application rather than on the details of the interface and the system.

These frameworks bring COOPERATION developers the advantages of object-oriented programming in an integrated, extensible environment.

MAJOR COMPONENTS: AN OVERVIEW

The components of COOPERATION are distributed into three platform-independent layers: The Desktop, the Application Layer, and the Services Layer (see Figure 2-4).

At the Desktop layer, the end user has icon-based control over the enterprise resources to which the user has access. The end user is also the beneficiary of the objects stored in the application layer, though these objects themselves may reside either in the desktop system or on the server. These applications include the business software provided with COOPERATION.

The services layer includes facilities that support enterprise-wide integration of data and applications. These facilities include many of the functions needed by the system administrator, but some are also accessed by end users.

In the next three sections, we will take a brief look at the contents of each of these layers.

ELEMENTS OF THE COOPERATION DESKTOP
The COOPERATION desktop is based on Microsoft Windows and Hewlett-Packard's NewWave GUI's. It not only combines the key features of both of these state-of-the-art windowing interfaces, it improves on them by extending their object orientations to extend the reach of the interfaces themselves into the heart of the enterprise's data.

Among the features of the COOPERATION's desktop that are most significant to the end user are the following:

- an office metaphor that gives the user a quick and easy way to map real-world experiences to the computer desktop

- desktop tools, including agents that are both programmable and teachable, assisting the user in automating repetitive tasks

- application integration that makes it easy for the user to bring legacy DOS applications into the COOPERATION environment.

Icons and Other GUI Components
Microsoft Windows hides the complexity and difficulty of a command-line DOS interface behind windows, icons, and pull-down menus. But icons in Windows can represent only applications or files; the user is not shielded from understanding the location, use, type, and other essential information about the objects represented by these icons. NewWave carries this process one level of abstraction closer to the user's experience. In NewWave, desktop icons are treated as objects. They do not represent applications and files but rather solutions and categories of working objects. Information and its associated activities can be represented in combination—in the best tradition of object-oriented programming—in NewWave objects.

COOPERATION works at the same level of abstraction as HP NewWave, but it adds tools that result in a well-integrated and easy-to-use desktop design.

The Office Metaphor
Figure 2-5 shows a typical COOPERATION desktop. As you can see, it includes a number of objects that relate directly to office workers' daily experiences: file drawers, folders, a waste basket, and in/out trays are the most obvious of these.

Users can design their own COOPERATION desktops to include whatever objects they work with most often and they can arrange these objects any way they like on the desktop. This includes not only the locations of icons on the desktop but also what is stored in what folders, how the various colors of folder tabs are used, what categories of folder will exist

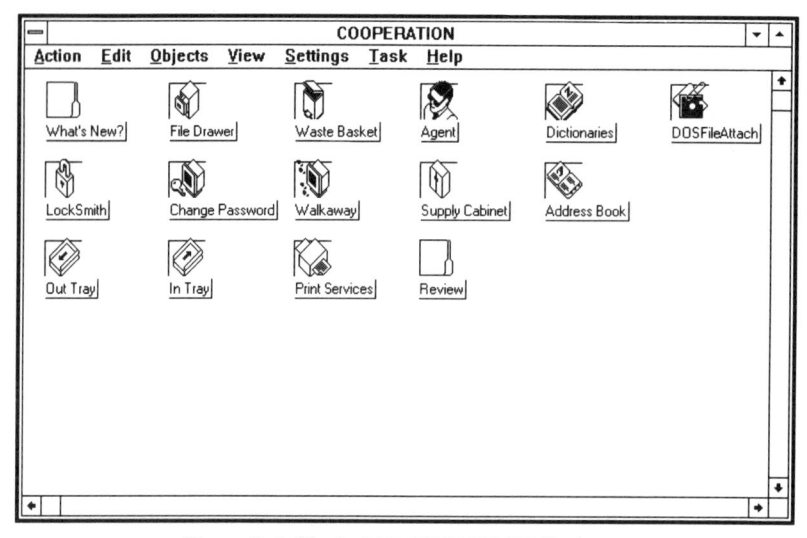

Figure 2-5: Typical COOPERATION Desktop

as master templates, and a host of other user-controllable aspects of the desktop.

MULTIPLE DESKTOPS

This ability to customize the desktop becomes particularly important when the user plays several different roles in an organization or is involved in multiple projects, products, or tasks. COOPERATION extends the NewWave desktop concept by permitting each user to maintain as many separate desktops as desired.

A bookkeeper in the accounting department, for example, might maintain one desktop for dealing with the issuance of checks to vendors, and another desktop for handling a task force assignment looking into how to make the processing of employee expense accounts more efficient. The application and document object groups needed in each desktop would almost certainly be quite different from one another. This bookkeeper might be dealing with vendor payments when another member of the task force sends an electronic mail message with a new idea for the expense account problem. Without missing a beat, the bookkeeper simply iconizes the check-writing desktop temporarily, opens the task force desktop, deals with the message, and then returns to the original desktop. Users can deal with situations this way without quitting applications, saving documents, or taking other steps that are necessary on systems that pre-date the object-oriented COOPERATION desktop.

Task Automation Tools

Most employees have one or more repetitive tasks they have to perform. These tasks may involve numerous individual steps that are invoked by choosing options from pull-down menus, opening objects by double-clicking on their icons, sending mail or printing documents by dragging icons representing these objects to an out tray or a printer object. COOPERATION permits the user to automate these tasks, even if they are fairly complex, through the creation of desktop agents. An agent can be created either by asking the agent task object to watch while a task is performed and to memorize it or by writing an agent task script.

As we will see in Chapter 4, scripting with the Agent Task Language (ATL) is a skill that is accessible to many end users. The ATL, combined with the ability to use point-and-click techniques to create interfaces for such scripts, makes it possible for users to design mini-applications for many categories of problem. While the ATL is not, strictly speaking, object-oriented, it does have a number of the benefits of an object-oriented environment that make it quite approachable and powerful.

DEGREES OF APPLICATION INTEGRATION

Application integration is available in four varieties, or levels, in COOPERATION, ranging from a basic registration that permits an application to be launched from the desktop through full integration. This last requires the author of the application to modify it to make it COOPERATION-compatible, but most of the other levels of integration can be created by a system administrator or end user without programming.

Details of all of these desktop-level functions and activities are provided in Chapter 3.

ELEMENTS OF THE COOPERATION APPLICATION ENVIRONMENT

COOPERATION includes several powerful business applications that go beyond the usual word processing, spreadsheet, and database applications typically already owned by a business enterprise. These applications include:

- group calendar
- compound document editor
- electronic mail
- business information monitor
- SQL query facility
- Remote Application Access (RAA)

We will look briefly at each of these applications in the following pages; Chapter 6 is devoted entirely to a fuller explanation of these applications and their operation.

GROUP CALENDAR

Every COOPERATION user is automatically part of a group calendaring process. This process focuses on the interaction of three different calendars (see Figure 2-6).

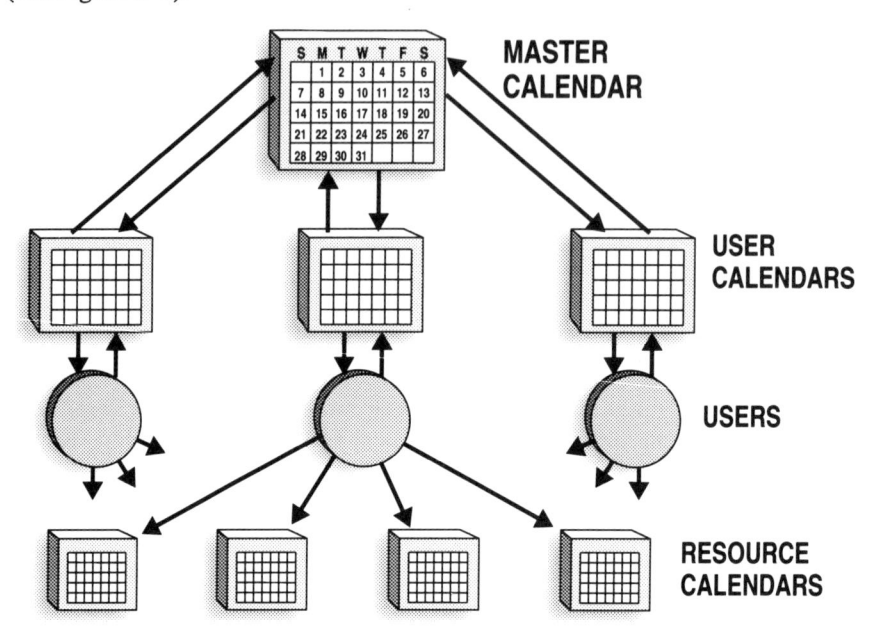

Figure 2-6: The Three COOPERATION Calendars

The Master Calendar keeps track of activities that affect a work group's needs to schedule meetings involving some or all of its members. Daily activities are generally recorded here. If a group member wishes to schedule a one-hour meeting for Tuesday at 3:30 p.m. with six other members of the group, the Master Calendar can be used to determine if that meeting conflicts with any activities those people have already scheduled.

Each user can maintain one or more calendars for project-related activities or for other purposes. These calendars will typically be used for keeping track of deadlines, project schedules and the like, rather than for appointments and meetings. Even if an appointment is related to a project, the user will generally post this information on the Master Calendar so that others in the group who wish to schedule time with the individual can do so.

There are also resource calendars, which enable users to schedule the availability of conference rooms, audio-visual lab equipment, demonstration systems, and the like.

As you will see in Chapter 6 when we discuss group calendars in more detail, individuals exercise total control over their schedules; a meeting cannot be "forced" on an individual even if a time slot is available. Instead, the calendar is closely linked to the mail system to coordinate invitations and responses.

COMPOUND DOCUMENT EDITOR

Because COOPERATION supports many object types, including text, graphics, and spreadsheets among others, it must provide a way for the user to integrate these various types of information into documents that can be mailed to other COOPERATION users, printed, and otherwise managed. The Compound Document Editor in COOPERATION provides this integration point. In its earliest release, COOPERATION includes a built-in editor for such documents. As third-party products such as AmiPro from Lotus begin to provide support for this capability, users will be able to integrate them into the COOPERATION to supplement or replace the built-in editor.

Figure 2-7 shows a prototypical compound document containing a text object (a letter), a spreadsheet object (part of a worksheet) and a graphic object (a drawing of the product being discussed).

A compound document is an instance of the abstract Compound Document Object. The user creates a new compound document by selecting the master object and "cloning" it. Formats for various kinds of compound documents can also be created as sub-classes of the Compound Document object so that instances of specifically formatted compound documents can be created quickly and easily. Business forms, regular reports, shareholder information, market analyses, product data sheets, and other such objects with relatively fixed formats can thus be dealt with quite effectively, even by users unfamiliar with their formatting rules.

Compound documents can be mailed to other COOPERATION users as a single object, which makes using them in a work group quite simple.

COOPERATION MAIL

The COOPERATION Mail system is designed to work with most major commercial mail systems. It also provides core functionality for other components of the COOPERATION application environment. For example, when someone in a work group wishes to schedule a meeting with several other members of the group, the request for the meeting is sent by COOPERATION Mail. This process is transparent to the user, who simply carries out the task of asking for a meeting; COOPERATION invokes the mail system behind the scenes for the user.

To send mail to other users in the group or elsewhere in the enterprise,

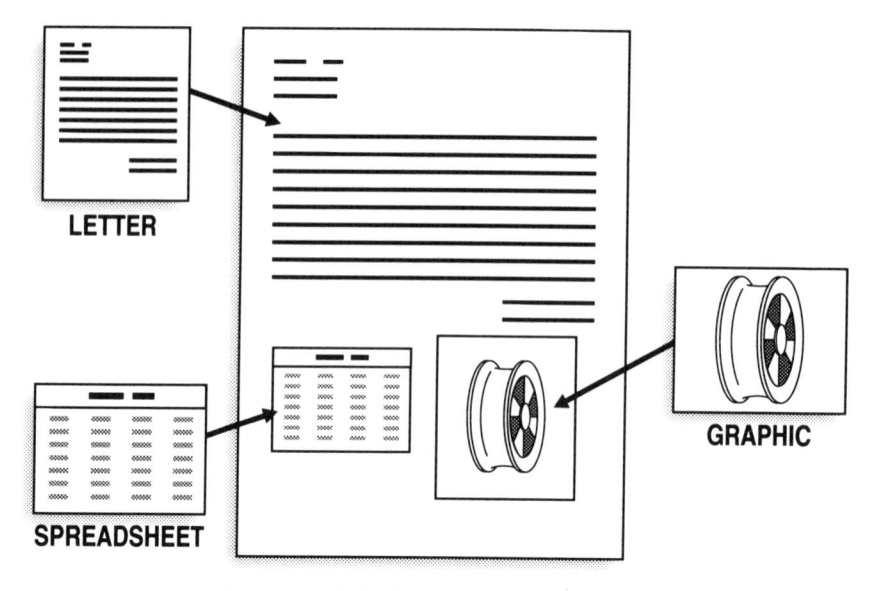

Figure 2-7: A Typical Compound Document

users simply place the objects to be mailed into their out tray. Incoming mail appears in the user's in tray. Each user can have one or more address books; these books are used automatically by COOPERATION Mail to address and route mail properly. The user simply provides the names of addressees and drops the object into the out tray; COOPERATION Mail handles the rest.

The mail system is enhanced by the inclusion of other useful objects, including:

- envelopes, into which multiple objects being sent to common addressees can be placed
- distribution lists, which streamline sending objects to groups which are frequent addressees of mail
- special forms for dealing with telephone messages

BUSINESS INFORMATION MONITOR

COOPERATION's Business Information Monitor (BIM) is designed to provide management at all levels of the enterprise with the ability to monitor, maintain, manage and report on the status of information contained in the enterprise's information network. Using BIM, the big picture of the organization can be presented to management so they can make informed decisions. It can help users turn raw data in spreadsheets, database files, and other sources into useful information. The timely use of this graphically presented information, in turn, can give an organization a significant competitive edge.

Information stored in a Lotus 1-2-3 or Microsoft Excel spreadsheet, or in any SQL or DB2 database, can be easily integrated into a BIM object. A collection of such objects permits a manager to see at a glance the status of critical measures of the enterprise or organization's status. Alarms can be set to notify the user when any of these critical measures reach or exceed user-defined threshold values.

Figure 2-8 shows a typical BIM view. It is set up to enable the user of this COOPERATION desktop to monitor the status and trends associated with the current ratio, inventory turns, and ROA values of the organization.

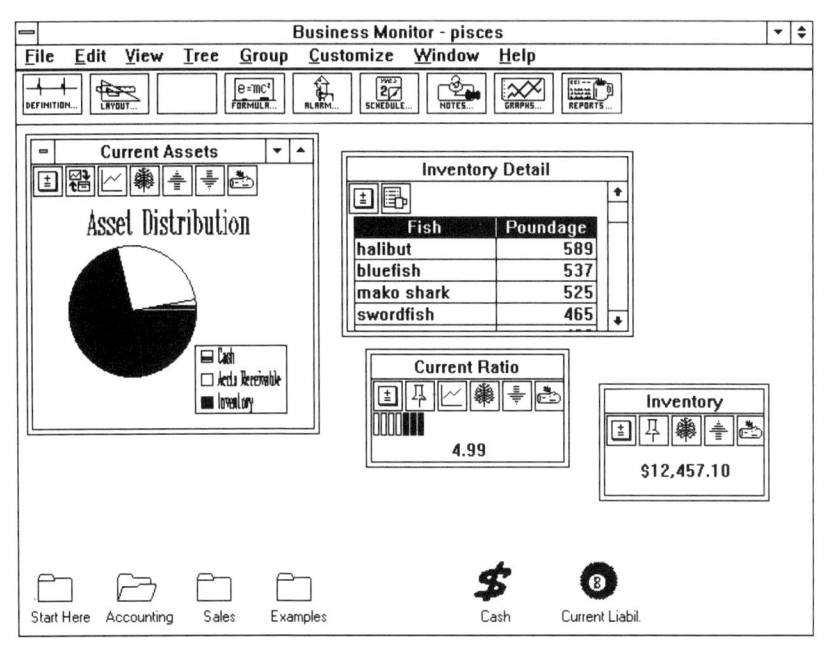

Figure 2-8: Typical BIM View

Users can "drill down" through the BIM objects to examine the raw data behind each monitor and view. Once a BIM object has been constructed, the user of that monitor or view needs to know nothing about where the data is stored in the enterprise, how it is obtained, or what its structure is. The manager simply looks at the manifestation of data in the form from which decisions can be made.

Not only can users view static data, they can also examine trends. Both static data and trends can be printed as well.

SQL QUERY FACILITY

A key element of the COOPERATION design is the ability of the user to gain transparent access to information stored in the enterprise database. In modern organizations, this database is typically composed of a number of separate tables and files, probably created using tools from several vendors. Most data is stored in database management systems (DBMS's) that can be programmed and controlled with Structured Query Language (SQL).

COOPERATION includes several applications that are COOPERATION-compliant so that they are tightly integrated into the environment. These tools, including SQLBase, an OS/2 relational database that resides on the COOPERATION server, make it possible for users to establish communication with, extract data from, and modify the contents of database files whose location and structure are unknown to them.

REMOTE APPLICATION ACCESS

The COOPERATION Remote Application Access (RAA) Manager facilitates the need for complex and *ad hoc* communication between the desktop user and information stored in applications residing on other systems. Essentially, the RAA Manager permits complex telecommunications processes such as dial-ups, log-ins and copying and pasting data to be automated into scripts, which can then be stored as objects represented by icons on the user's desktop.

Users can thus carry out even complex data-gathering operations, perhaps involving the necessity of logging into more than one remote computer system, without specific knowledge of either the location of the data or of the log-in process.

The RAA Manager supports a host of terminal emulation protocols and binary transfer protocols. Users experience the RAA Manager as collections of related terminal and edit windows encapsulating and containing scripts. Function key mapping is another key aspect of the RAA Manager's role in the COOPERATION application environment.

Chapter 6 discusses the application aspects of COOPERATION in greater detail.

ELEMENTS OF THE COOPERATION SERVICES LAYER

COOPERATION includes a number of groups of applications designed to provide cross-application and system management services. This group of applications collectively makes up the services layer. The services, which are discussed in detail in Chapter 7, can be broken down into the following four broad categories:

- information services
- document management services

- software supply services
- system management services

COOPERATION INFORMATION SERVICES

Information is the heart of a business enterprise. Its access and management are, in turn, at the heart of COOPERATION. The information services component of the services layer includes applications that provide:

- transparent database access
- file storage and retrieval
- full-text search and retrieval of key information
- document conversion

COOPERATION provides transparent database access to other aspects of the environment. These are services that are provided transparently to the user and used automatically by other aspects of COOPERATION that require access to database information to carry out their tasks. We will have much more to say about SQL and database access in Chapter 7.

The COOPERATION Information Storage Manager (ISM) facilitates the storage and retrieval of files and documents throughout the enterprise information network. To the end user, the primary benefit of the ISM is the ability to avoid the necessity of recalling detailed information about files. The ISM manages the location, storage, and retrieval of specific individual files, thus enabling the widespread sharing of information in the enterprise.

ISM includes a number of useful facilities that are detailed in Chapter 8. One of the most unusual and helpful of these facilities is the version pro-files that uniquely identify each version of a file.

Documents managed by ISM can be retrieved based on:

- title
- creator
- last modifier
- creation date
- last-modified date
- keywords

An enterprise can choose to extend the facilities of the ISM by the addition of the optional Text Retrieval engine. This application permits users to retrieve text-based files on the basis of their text content rather than on any of the criteria listed above. The user queries the system for all documents that contain specific words or phrases (or even for documents that do not contain specific words or phrases). The Text Retrieval engine then searches all indexed areas of the system—subject to user control and security provisions—and finds all qualifying documents. A profile of each document is returned to the user, who can then choose which document(s) to retrieve in their entirety.

Many enterprises use multiple word processors, particularly across department lines. Moving information between departments or work groups that use different word processors has been a problem for all modern enterprises that have not imposed a single word processing standard throughout the organization. COOPERATION addresses the need to allow different departments with different document needs to use different word processors by providing document conversion. Transparent to the user, incoming documents that may have been created in one word processor are translated into the user's word processor format, including text and formatting.

Figure 2-9 shows the degree to which document conversion is important in the COOPERATION environment. A number of system-level services take advantage of this functionality.

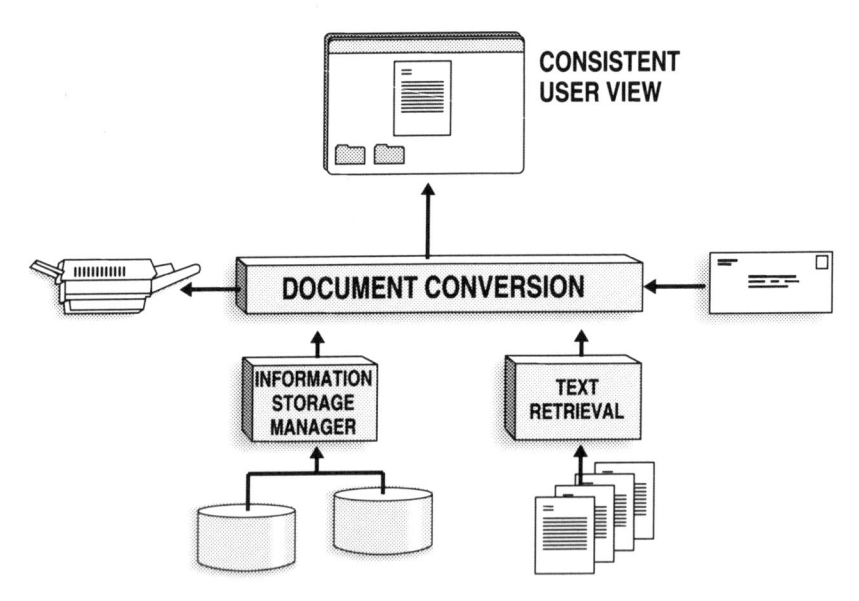

Figure 2-9: Document Conversion Usage

Because the COOPERATION Mail system takes advantage of document conversion, users who use different word processors can send each other mail created in their word processors without being concerned about the readability or format of the document on the receiving end.

One of the most difficult problems for modern enterprises is the

management of applications that are intended for use by several users in the organization. Buying a sufficient number of copies to permit everyone who ever needs the application results in inefficient and costly site licenses or over-purchase of software. Ensuring that usage complies with licenses signed with software vendors can become a serious waste of resources.
COOPERATION solves these problems with a server-based Supply Cabinet.

The system administrator installs copies of shared applications into the Supply Cabinet, determines which users on the network can check these applications in and out, and then lets the system handle the rest of the management. The Supply Cabinet ensures, for example, that no more than the number of users for which the organization is authorized can use a particular application at one time. This approach also means that upgrading software is greatly facilitated because all copies of the program exist in one place.

Finally, the COOPERATION services layer includes a number of applications to assist the system administrator in each work group. These facilities enable system administrators to carry out routine tasks such as:

- adding and removing workstations
- adding and removing users
- modifying group-related access privileges
- controlling external data access
- managing shared applications with the Supply Cabinet

All of these facilities are provided through the same COOPERATION desktop the system administrator uses for non-administrative tasks. This makes the use of administrative facilities much easier and more familiar than typical system administrator facilities.

SECURITY IN COOPERATION

COOPERATION security is characterized by flexibility and user involvement.

Many kinds of documents—text-only, compound, database, and application-specific—are maintained in a business enterprise. Many systems force system administrators to impose a uniform security system on documents in arbitrary groups regardless of the sensitivity of the information contained in them. COOPERATION, through its document management facility and the Information Storage Manager (ISM), allows each document to have its own security access control. Further, these controls can provide various users with different levels of access to documents. This flexible security scheme means that the enterprise can assign access restrictions based on realistic enterprise needs rather than on the arbitrary limits imposed by the software managing such access.

Beyond that flexibility, however, COOPERATION differs from traditional security control systems in permitting the author or owner of a document to play a key role in determining access privileges. Without involving the system administrator and without the arbitrariness of most software-based security systems, a user can determine who should be able to have what kind of access to documents created on the local desktop, even when those documents are stored on the server.

Of course, the enterprise that ultimately owns the information can, through the system administrator, make overriding decisions about security of specific documents despite the initial thoughts of the creators of such information.

Objects and even the workstation itself, can be secured with passwords in much the same way as documents. These passwords are, in turn, objects that have such characteristics as:

- minimum length
- minimum and maximum age
- forced logoff based on time or password attempts

COOPERATION AS AN OPEN SYSTEM

Because it is designed to be an open system, COOPERATION takes on a different form in each organization. Each enterprise will integrate DOS and other Windows and NewWave applications into the COOPERATION environment to varying degrees depending on the nature of legacy systems and on growth plans.

As new applications are purchased and established software is integrated increasingly tightly into the COOPERATION world, the utility and flexibility of COOPERATION as a work environment will change from the user's perspective. But by proper integration, all of these changes can be easily absorbed by users who see everything through the COOPERATION desktop GUI.

3
The COOPERATION Desktop

This chapter describes the major concept embodied in the COOPERATION desktop, the office metaphor. Next, it describes the primary objects you'll see in COOPERATION: desktops, icons, and templates. This discussion includes information on how to create new instances of such objects. The chapter then describes the tools available in the COOPERATION environment that are accessible from the desktop. One of the most powerful ideas in COOPERATION is that of multiple desktops. This chapter discusses how users can create and use several COOPERATION desktops to make their work more efficient. It also discusses the power and utility of the Object Management Facility (OMF).

THE OFFICE METAPHOR IN COOPERATION

The COOPERATION Desktop provides the user with a familiar frame of reference for dealing with objects by patterning itself on the model of a typical office. As we saw in Chapter 2, this includes providing icons that resemble file cabinets, drawers, files, and other familiar office objects. As a result of the adoption of this metaphor, users quickly become familiar and comfortable with their electronic environment.

MANIPULATING OBJECTS

Icons on the COOPERATION Desktop actually represent both office objects and tools. One special type of office object is the folder. Folders are used to organize other objects. In COOPERATION, the user can create new folders and take advantage of a color-coding scheme to help organize information into categories. Folders and other objects can, in turn, be stored in file drawers.

Tools are a special type of object. They typically have one of two purposes. Many tools provide a common, generic point for all applications and objects accessible from the desktop to access services elsewhere in COOPERATION. Other tools are applications which either do not always create objects as part of their role (such as file utilities) or for which no defined integration into COOPERATION yet exists. In the latter case, these tool objects are generally either utilities or applications.

Users can drag object icons over tool icons and apply the tool's service to that object. This is true regardless of which application you are using and where the tool resides on the COOPERATION network.

Figure 3-1 shows a COOPERATION desktop with several types of object represented by icons. These icons encapsulate compound documents, worksheets, project plans, and other similar items along with the software required to manipulate them.

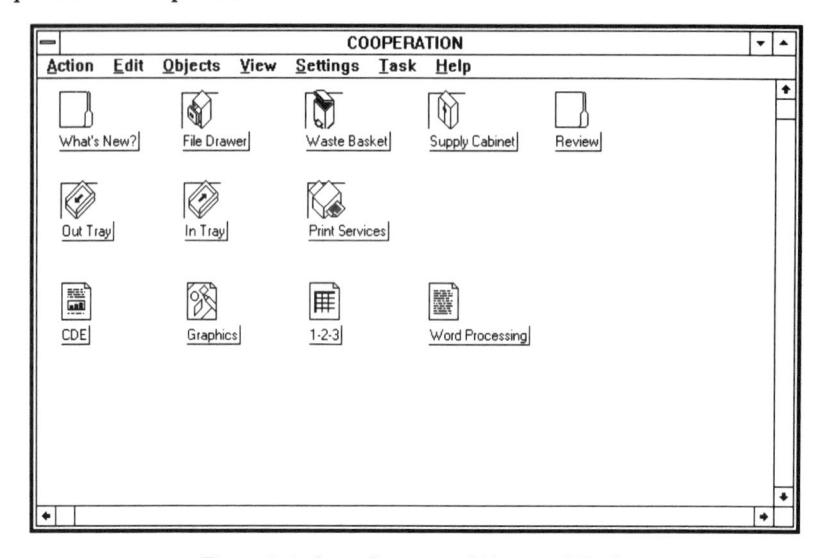

Figure 3-1: Icons Represent Objects and Tools

Users move objects by manipulating their icons with a mouse: pointing, clicking, double-clicking, and dragging. For example, a document can be printed by dragging its icon to the icon representing the Printers tool.

CREATING NEW OBJECTS

The user almost always works with objects in COOPERATION, not with files and applications as with more traditional application environments. (The exception to this rule results from the lack of tight integration of some existing programs into COOPERATION.) Creating what has traditionally been referred to as a new "document" within Cooperation, then, involves creating a new object that encapsulates the data and information about the application that manages that type of data.

To create a new object, the user chooses the "Create a New..." option from the "Objects" menu. This produces a dialog that displays an icon for each type of object it is possible to create on this desktop. These icons typically include various types of data documents related to both Windows and DOS applications, database queries, compound documents, and other COOPERATION-specific types of objects. Simply by clicking on the desired object type's icon and giving the new instance of that object a name, the user creates a new object.

This notion of inherited object types goes one level deeper in

COOPERATION: many object types can have sub-types, called "masters" which have additional characteristics beyond those contained in the object type itself. For example, Figure 3-2 shows the "Create a New" dialog in which the user has begun to create an instance of a Folder object. Notice that there are several master types of folders, in this case reflecting the user's ability to define a folder tab's color. The user can give the object a name and not select a master type, thereby creating a generic folder object or click on one of the master types and change the color of the tab.

Users could go yet one step farther by defining their own new types of masters. For example, a user could create a folder containing several blank documents which, taken together, are usually needed to support project management. They could then ask COOPERATION to remember this as a new master type. Thereafter, they could create additional copies of this object by choosing the folder object in the "Create A New..." dialog and then selecting the newly defined master. COOPERATION would then create a new project folder, complete with the necessary start-up documents.

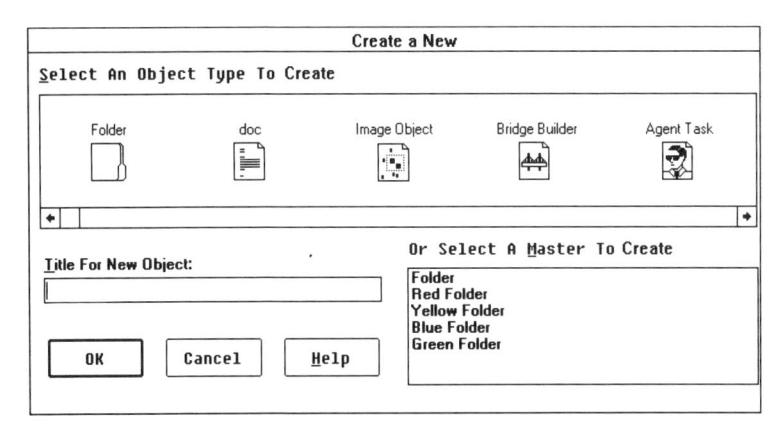

Figure 3-2: Creating a New Object and Master Instance

PRIMARY OBJECTS IN THE GUI

In addition to icons that represent objects and tools, there are two other primary objects in the COOPERATION environment:

- desktops
- menus

COOPERATION DESKTOPS

COOPERATION users can create and maintain as many desktop objects as they wish. A desktop object can be thought of as encapsulating a collection of other COOPERATION objects—documents and tools, for example—that the user sees as all being related to a particular task. The ability to maintain multiple desktops is a powerful object-oriented concept that is unique to COOPERATION (see Figure 3-3).

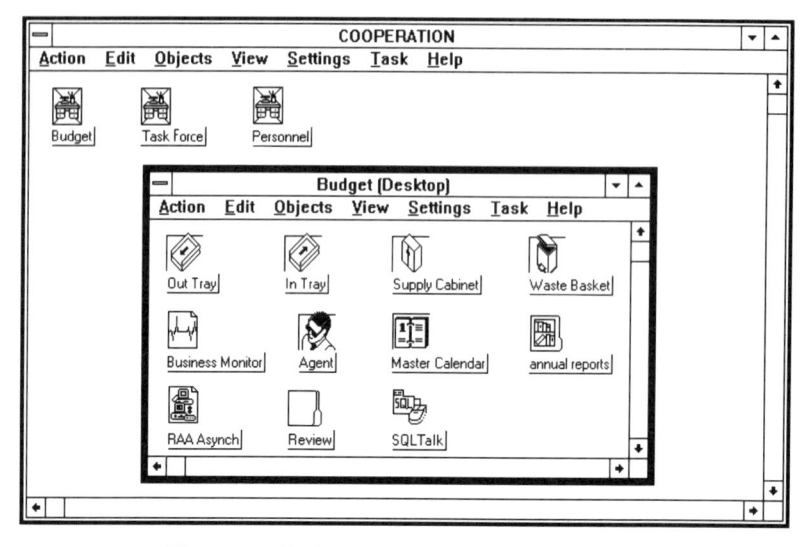

Figure 3-3: Each User Can Have Many Desktops

For example, an assistant manager in the Operations group might be called upon to prepare a budget, write a personnel evaluation, schedule production review meetings, and serve on an inter-departmental task force. This user could create a separate desktop for each of these sets of tasks. The budget-related desktop might only need a worksheet icon encapsulating a spreadsheet application and the worksheet on which the budget is being prepared. The personnel evaluation desktop, on the other hand, might need links to corporate databases as well as a word processor.

A COOPERATION user can have only one desktop active at one time, but all of the desktops in a user's environment can be immediately accessible at the click of a mouse. Our hypothetical assistant manager might be working diligently away on the spreadsheet when a member of the task force calls to ask that a follow-up note be sent to two non-members. The assistant manager simply collapses the budget desktop to an icon, opens the task force desktop from its icon to full-screen size, and carries out the request. When the task is done, the budget desktop can be opened with the same facility. Desktops remember between sessions what application and documents were active last, even when the user leaves COOPERATION or shuts down the system.

MENUS

Most of the operations users perform in COOPERATION are carried out either by manipulating icons or by selecting options from one of the many menus in COOPERATION windows. Figure 3-4 shows a typical COOPERATION Desktop menu bar. As you can see, it contains seven menus:

- **Action**, where users instruct COOPERATION to do something such as lock their desktops while they are away, launch a DOS program, or close the desktop
- **Edit**, where users cut, copy, paste, and otherwise manipulate objects on the Desktop
- **Objects**, which includes options that allow users to create new objects, open and print existing objects, import and export objects, and undertake other object-related tasks
- **View**, where users control the appearance of the desktop and the way objects are displayed (in a list that is arranged according to their directions or iconically) and arranged
- **Settings**, from which the user can control which tools appear on the desktop, which master objects appear in the dialog from which new objects are created and what order they appear, the user's name and password, and the time zone in which the workstation is located
- **Task**, which permits the user to create, manage, and perform automated tasks (about which we will have more to say in the next chapter)
- **Help**, where the user can get context-sensitive and general help running COOPERATION

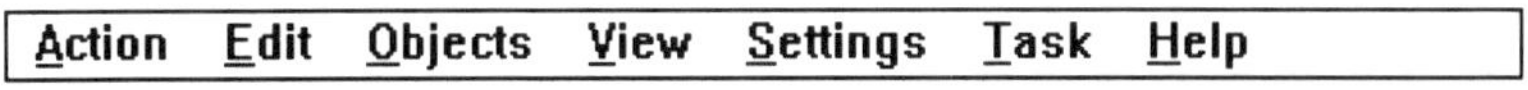

| Action | Edit | Objects | View | Settings | Task | Help |

Figure 3-4: Menu Bar on NCR COOPERATION Desktop

AVAILABLE TOOLS

Tools can be distinguished from other objects on the COOPERATION Desktop by the appearance they give of being embedded into the desktop surface. Figure 3-3 shows a portion of a typical desktop. The document object's icon appears to be lying on top of the desktop's surface while the Waste Basket's tool icon appears embedded in the desktop in 3-D style. All tools have the appearance of the Waste Basket (with different icons for various tools, of course).

When users create new COOPERATION desktops, they can choose

from a variety of tools to place on the desktop. Each desktop can and should have its own set of tools that relate to the tasks for which it is designed. Among the two dozen or so tools available, the more commonly used ones are:

- waste basket
- file drawer
- printers
- agent
- DOS file attach
- "Walkaway"
- in and out trays
- Master Calendar

Users can add these tools to their desktops—and also remove them if desired—any time. The "Manage Tools..." option on the "Settings" menu (see Figure 3-5) provides access to the full complement of tools available in a given COOPERATION installation. Many third-party software developers are creating tools to be added to the COOPERATION desktop.

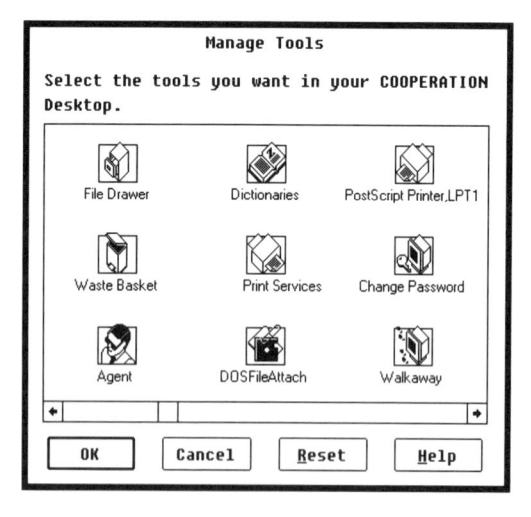

Figure 3-5. Managing Tools on the COOPERATION Desktop

When a desktop is not presently in use, it can be collapsed to an iconic view, where it remains available to be reactivated with a double-click of the mouse. The work going on in the desktop isn't terminated, it is simply suspended. This means that the amount of time users lose switching between desktops is minimized.

A desktop is like any other object. It is created by choosing the "Create a New..." option from the "Objects" menu in the COOPERATION top-level desktop. One of the objects in the resulting dialog is a desktop object type (see Figure 3-6). By double-clicking on this object and giving the new desktop a name, the user creates a new desktop. The default desktop is empty, but as with all objects, it would be possible to create a new master type of desktop that contained a default set of tools and/or objects. The user can quickly and easily "fill" the new desktop with objects and tools.

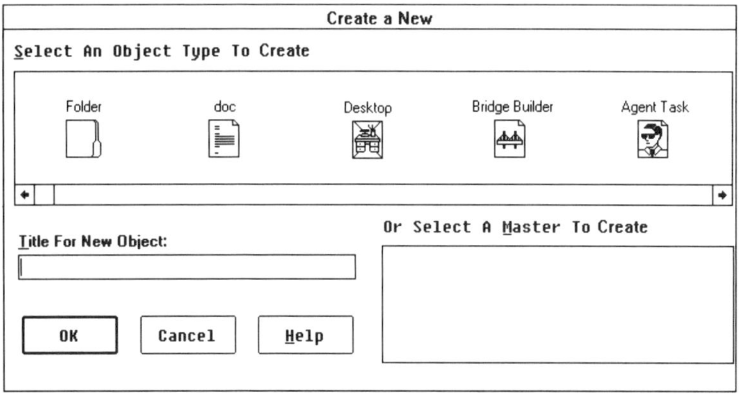

Figure 3-6: Creating a New Desktop

Most COOPERATION users who work with multiple desktops have most or all of their desktops available and minimized to icons all the time. This facilitates switching between tasks.

Some objects may be relevant in more than one desktop situation. Depending on the interdependence of the objects and their contents, the user can have the same object on more than one desktop in two ways. The object can be copied and pasted, which creates a separate copy of the object on both desktops. Changes to one version of the object's data will not be reflected in the other desktop's version. But if the user really only wants one copy of the object in the environment but wishes to access it from more than one desktop, the object can be shared. This process is virtually identical to copying: the user selects the object, chooses the "Share" option from the "Edit" menu, then activates the other desktop and chooses "Paste" from the same menu. This time, rather than a copy of the original object, each desktop has access to a single copy of the data.

COOPERATION keeps track of the object's status. If the user opens the object on one desktop and doesn't close it before attempting to access it from another desktop, the document's icon will be dimmed and will not respond to mouse clicks.

THE OBJECT MANAGEMENT FACILITY

Keeping track of connections within and between objects in COOPERATION is the task of the Object Management Facility (OMF). This application manages all of the details entailed by the object-oriented design of the desktop interface, including:

- starting the correct application program when the user selects a particular type of data object
- providing a consistent method of combining information of different types in compound documents
- keeping track of objects' containers (such as file folders and drawers)

The OMF works primarily through a special directory facility atop the MS-DOS file system. All object data files and executable program files are stored in conventional MS-DOS files. The OMF creates and manages file names for the data files that are part of an object, providing this information to the appropriate application when it is started. The user always refers to objects by meaningful names and never deals with the details of the names or locations of the underlying files.

There are three types of links in the OMF. Information links are connections between objects that permit them to share a single data source. Data passing links facilitate the passing of information between objects. Visual, or display, links permit an application to provide a view of data belonging to another application.

DESKTOP AGENTS AND THE AGENT TASK LANGUAGE

One of the most powerful ideas COOPERATION brings to the modern office is the notion of meaningful automation of repetitive and complex tasks. It provides these facilities in the form of agent tasks and menu tasks. The difference between these two types of tasks lies in how users perform and manage them, not in the kinds of actions they can automate.

In general, agent tasks are suitable for large, project-oriented tasks that span several objects. Agent tasks can also be scheduled through the agent scheduler to take place at a certain time or repeatedly on time-triggered events.

Menu tasks, on the other hand, are usually best for short tasks that are confined to a single window object and to objects it contains. (A third type of task, called a tool task, enables you to do some keystroke-macro recording in DOS applications. We will not examine this type of task in this book.)

CREATING AND PERFORMING TASKS

Users can create either type of task two ways: by recording the task (performing it while COOPERATION records the user's actions and remembers them for replay) or by editing a script using the COOPERATION Agent Task Language (ATL). In fact, these two approaches are not mutually exclu-sive: a user might record a task and then edit its script later, either because the requirement for the task changed or because some other functionality is required. Another point of connection between the two approaches lies in the fact that beginning scripters often use recording as a technique to see what the ATL scripts should look like, to learn the language, and then later use ATL more frequently than the recording technique.

When users record their actions as a task to be performed later, COOPERATION keeps track of most of their actions from the time they start recording until they turn it off. At that point, the task is compiled and stored appropriately depending on whether it's an agent task or a menu task. While recording is in process (see Figure 3-7), each line of ATL generated by the user's actions is displayed in the window containing the task script. Some actions, such as moving the pointer, viewing a menu without choosing an option from it, canceling a dialog, and getting on-line help, are not recorded because they are not viewed as significant to the process being "learned" by COOPERATION.

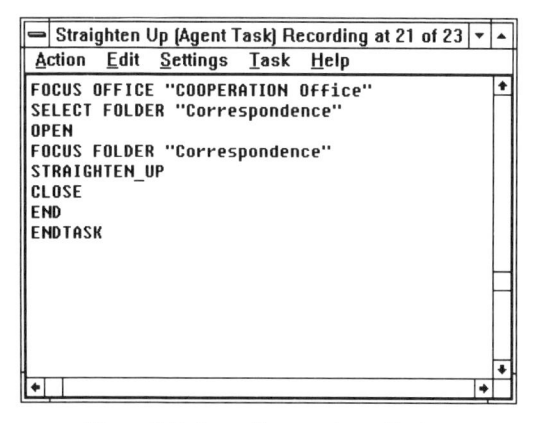

```
Straighten Up [Agent Task] Recording at 21 of 23
Action  Edit  Settings  Task  Help
FOCUS OFFICE "COOPERATION Office"
SELECT FOLDER "Correspondence"
OPEN
FOCUS FOLDER "Correspondence"
STRAIGHTEN_UP
CLOSE
END
ENDTASK
```

Figure 3-7: Recording an Agent Script

Menu tasks can be added to the Task menu in the window of the object to which they belong. This makes them easy to execute; they are like any other menu option. Agent tasks are executed by dragging their icons to the Agent tool.

Since agent tasks are objects, creating them begins the same way as creating all other COOPERATION objects: by selecting the Agent Task icon from the dialog that appears when the user selects "Create a New..." from the "Objects" menu. Once an agent task has been created and saved, the user simply opens its icon, starts recording by choosing the appropriate "Action" menu entry, carries out the processes to be recorded, and then chooses "Stop Recording" from the "Action" menu. The task is then ready to be carried out by dragging its icon to the Agent Task tool icon on the desktop.

Menu tasks are not, strictly speaking, objects. They more closely resemble properties of their containing window objects. To create a menu task, the user chooses "Create Menu Task..." from the "Task" menu. This results in a dialog like the one shown in Figure 3-8. The user gives the task a name, supplies comments if desired, and determines how to store and invoke the task.

Menu tasks can be invoked by the user choosing them from the menu if they are added to it with the checkbox in the dialog shown in Figure 3-8. Each object's window can also have one menu task that automatically executes any time the window is opened. Menu tasks that neither appear on a menu nor autostart can be activated by the user choosing "Perform Menu Task..." from the "Task" menu.

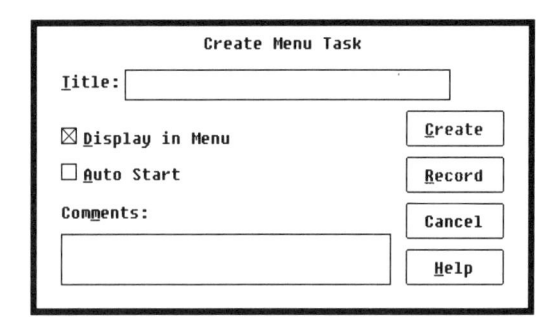

Figure 3-8: Menu Task Dialog

SCHEDULING AGENT TASKS

COOPERATION includes an agent calendar through which you can schedule agent tasks to execute at certain times on certain dates. This calendar has some of the same features as the Group Calendar discussed in Chapter 6, but it is used only for scheduling tasks to be carried out by agents.

The agent calendar is associated, logically enough, with the Agent

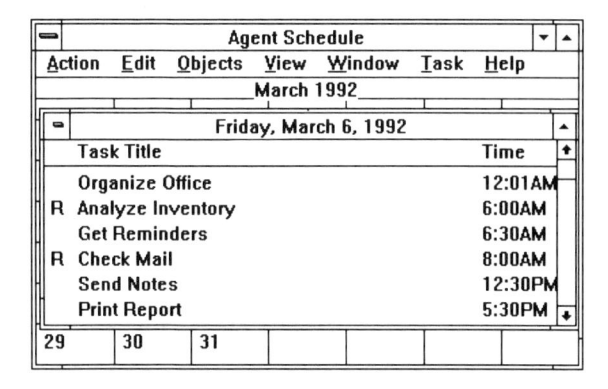

```
┌─────────────────────────────────────────────────┐
│ ═                  Agent Schedule        ▼ ▲    │
│ Action  Edit  Objects  View  Window  Task  Help │
│                    March 1992                   │
│ ┌─────────────────────────────────────────────┐ │
│ │ ▄          Friday, March 6, 1992        ▲   │ │
│ │ Task Title                        Time  ♦   │ │
│ │ Organize Office                   12:01AM   │ │
│ │ R Analyze Inventory               6:00AM    │ │
│ │ Get Reminders                     6:30AM    │ │
│ │ R Check Mail                      8:00AM    │ │
│ │ Send Notes                        12:30PM   │ │
│ │ Print Report                      5:30PM ▼  │ │
│ │ 29 │ 30 │ 31 │    │    │    │               │ │
│ └─────────────────────────────────────────────┘ │
└─────────────────────────────────────────────────┘
```

Figure 3-9: Agent Calendar with Tasks

Tool. Figure 3-9 shows a page from the agent calendar, with some tasks open in it.

To schedule an agent task, the user simply copies or cuts the task, opens the agent calendar, pastes the task into the calendar, and chooses the date and time at which the task should be performed. Tasks can be carried out once or repetitively. If the user asks to schedule a task repetitively, another dialog (see Figure 3-10) appears in which the regularity of the task

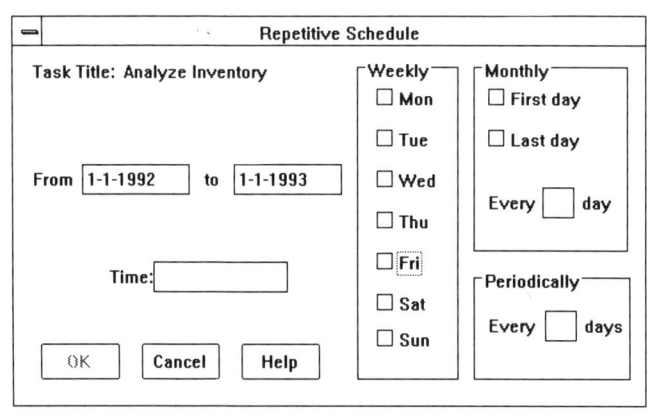

```
┌───────────────────────────────────────────────────────┐
│ ─                   Repetitive Schedule               │
│                                                       │
│ Task Title: Analyze Inventory   ┌Weekly─┐ ┌Monthly──┐ │
│                                 │ ☐ Mon │ │☐First day│ │
│                                 │ ☐ Tue │ │☐Last day │ │
│ From │1-1-1992│ to │1-1-1993│   │ ☐ Wed │ │          │ │
│                                 │ ☐ Thu │ │Every │ │day│ │
│        Time: │          │       │ ☐ Fri │ └─────────┘ │
│                                 │ ☐ Sat │ ┌Periodically┐│
│                                 │ ☐ Sun │ │Every│ │days││
│    │ OK │  │Cancel│  │Help│     └───────┘ └──────────┘ │
└───────────────────────────────────────────────────────┘
```

Figure 3-10: Repetitive Task Scheduling

can be defined. The agent calendar then takes care of handling all of the date calculations and scheduling the task repetitively over the period defined by the user.

37

COMPLEX TASK AUTOMATION

Even fairly complex tasks involving network access, file transfer, mail and other processes that normally require user intervention can be converted into tasks that any user, regardless of training or experience, can carry out with a simple mouse click or menu selection.

Agents can even send messages to other agents. A rudimentary form of workflow automation could thus be carried out with such agent scripts, as depicted in Figure 3-11.

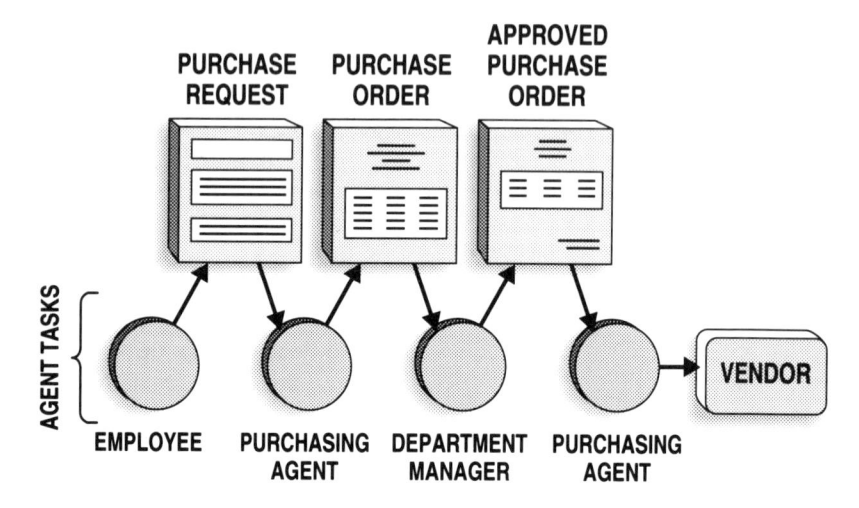

Figure 3-11: An Example of Task Automation.

4
Scripting the COOPERATION Desktop

The increasing demands being placed on business by today's era of rapid change have brought enormous pressures to bear on Information Services (IS) departments. Ever more complex solutions to broader and broader problems must be tackled using techniques that often extend the time it takes to design and develop the appropriate software. Object-oriented programming holds a great deal of hope for alleviating at least a large part of this problem.

Another approach to dealing with this crisis in software is to put more programming power into the hands of end users. There is much debate concerning whether most programming can eventually be done by relatively untrained end users. It has, however, become abundantly clear in recent years that end users can and will learn scripting languages and other accessible approaches to controlling their systems. COOPERATION provides end users access to scripting tools at several different points. This chapter focuses on desktop scripting with the NewWave Agent Task Language (ATL), but scripting support is also available in the Remote Application Access (RAA) Manager and in the Communications Authoring Tool (CAT).

We will begin this chapter with a discussion of the kind of background or skills necessary to undertake scripting in the ATL. We will then discuss the kinds of problems that can be successfully and efficiently addressed with scripts rather than full applications developed in formal programming languages. Next, we'll take an overview look at the ATL itself and at the Interface Builder that enables users to create Windows-style interfaces to their scripts. We will conclude the chapter with a discussion of an abbreviated methodology for the design and deployment of COOPERATION Desktop scripts, including some hints and tips to make such scripting projects successful and useful.

WHO CAN SCRIPT THE COOPERATION DESKTOP?

To answer the question of who can (or should attempt to) script activities in the COOPERATION Desktop, we must first review the two levels at which scripting can take place.

Virtually any user with a basic understanding of how they perform a particular task can create a script by recording mouse and keyboard actions. This process is identical to that used in some spreadsheet and word processing programs for the creation of macros. The user simply turns on the recording process, carries out a series of actions for which the user wants a script to be created, and then turns off the recorder. The task can then be saved and used later.

The other type of scripting, which will be the focus of most of this chapter's attention, involves creating a script from scratch using the powerful ATL, or editing a previously recorded script to change the data on which it operates or to add functionality to it. We call the user who will be comfortable with this process an Inventive User. Such people are characterized by:

- a desire and willingness to make their computer systems behave differently or solve highly individualistic problems
- a willingness to expend a certain amount of energy to gain that control
- a lack of interest in becoming a full-fledged programmer just to gain that control

Such users often write spreadsheet and word processing macros and may well have experimented with (or even made extensive use of) such scripting tools as Spinnaker PLUS and Asymetrix ToolBook. They may also have some experience writing programs in dBASE-like database products.

There is widespread disagreement about the differences, if any, between scripting and programming. One of the authors has spent several years studying scripting environments and how users experience them (see, for example, Shafer's *Complete Book of HyperTalk 2*, Addison-Wesley, 1991, as well as *The Shafer Report*, a monthly newsletter for Inventive Users). Based on that experience, we believe there are some important differences between the two approaches to application creation. These differences are summarized in Figure 4-1. We discuss each of these differences in the following paragraphs.

Learning: Scripting languages are usually "layered." That is, they either allow scripters to ease into their use by enabling them to accomplish useful and interesting work without mastering the entire language and environment, or they are supported by macro recording environments in which the user can learn the scripting language. Programming languages, on the other hand, tend to be things one needs to "swallow whole." Until a person has learned most of a programming language's syntax, structure, architecture, and syntax (if not vocabulary), it is difficult to accomplish any work which the end user would characterize as useful or interesting.

Complexity: Scripts tend to be small, single-purpose, and easily digested. This stems in part from their generally event-driven nature. A script is usually activated in response to a user-generated event. Users tend to think

	SCRIPTING	PROGRAMMING
Learning	Layered access	All-or-none
Complexity	Small & simple	Large & complex
Resources	Surface resources	Access to system
Speed	Slow (interpreted)	Fast (compiled)
Language	English-like	Compressed, cryptic
Editors	Basic functions	Full-function
Tools	Minimal	Extensive

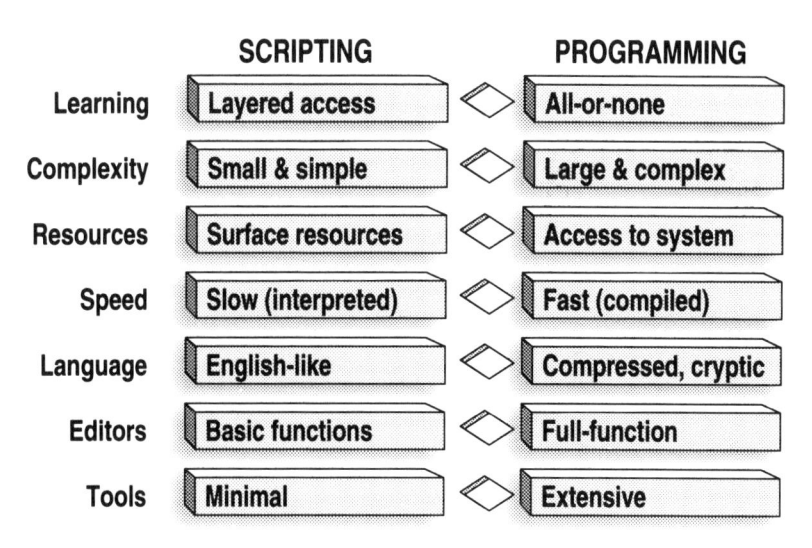

Figure 4-1: Scripting vs. Programming

of tasks as somewhat discrete objects. Most scripts, therefore, tend to be created in response to a need for a specific and singular task. Programs, on the other hand, are generally large, multi-purpose, and monolithic. This significant increase in complexity means that the creation, comprehension, and management of programs built with conventional programming languages tend to require a good deal of specialized training and experience.

Resource Access: Scripting environments are typically designed to insulate the scripter from low-level details of the operating system and graphic user interface on which the scripts will be run. This also means that the scripter cannot generally gain the same access to some levels of control of the interface and interaction with the system as a programming language.

Speed: Applications built using scripting tools generally execute more slowly than the same program would if it were written in a conventional compiled language like C or Pascal. Most scripting languages are interpreted, rather than compiled, which is a partial explanation of this fact. Even those scripting environments that include some form of compilation tend not to be very efficient at the process because it just isn't what the people who design and build scripting tools are best at doing.

Language: Scripting languages generally have smaller sets of instructions and those instructions tend to be named in a more English-like syntax than those in programming languages. For example, in a scripting language, one might find a command like "add 1 to total." This same command would be expressed in Pascal as "total := total + 1" and in C even more cryptically as "i++" or "++i" depending on the circumstances. There are dozens of other, similar examples. As a result, scripting languages feel more accessible to end users who are not trained programmers. (This has a subtle negative consequence as well, which we will address shortly.)

Editors: The editors that come with scripting tools tend to be simpler and less sophisticated than those with conventional programming languages. This is due, in part, to the fact that the scripter usually doesn't have to know much about the syntax and structure of programs to get things to work. Even though most scripting languages include programming ideas like control constructs, repeat loops, and other more advanced features, many people write numerous successful scripts without delving into these details. In scripting environments where code layout (indentation, etc.) is important, the editor usually handles such tasks fairly automatically.

Tools: Development tools for multiple programmers, multiple-file projects, and management of large scale projects are generally part of a traditional language tool like Pascal or C. Optionally, these capabilities can be acquired from a number of third-party suppliers. Scripting tools, on the other hand, tend to be focused on the single scripter and do not have support for things like keeping track of the latest versions of several different forms of an application.

There are many other differences between scripting and programming. (If you are interested in this subject, see Dan Shafer's *Scripting the Personal Computer*, In Press, The Reader Network: Redwood City, CA).

WHEN TO SCRIPT, WHEN TO PROGRAM

From what we have just said, it should be fairly clear that both the Desktop ATL scripting and the object-oriented programming frameworks available for COOPERATION have a place.

If you aren't a programmer, don't want to become one, and have a small number of specialized needs you'd like to meet, you'll choose scripting. If you are a trained or experienced programmer, your choice is not so clear-cut. You might well want to choose the ATL as a development environment for mini-applications that meet the following criteria:

- small number of users (little or no impact on enterprise)
- execution speed not critical
- compliance with UI standards can be loose
- focused task that you should be able to program by yourself in a reasonable amount of time
- task can be accomplished without low-level system resource access

The biggest single advantage of using scripting for such applications is speed of development. Scripting environments like the one that comes with the COOPERATION Desktop come with user interface construction tools, which saves a significant amount of design and coding time. They aren't compiled, so there is no finger-tapping time waiting for the next big compilation to finish.

On the other hand, when you need speed or access to low-level resources or the task is too large or has too many implications for the business to be handled at the scripting desktop level, then you should use OO techniques and the COOPERATION frameworks to create stand-alone applications that work well in the COOPERATION environment.

AN OVERVIEW OF THE ATL

The ATL embedded in COOPERATION is quite powerful and flexible, yet it offers users at all levels of experience and interest some capability they will find useful. Figure 2-4 shows a sample scripting session. Users who don't desire to program or to understand scripting can simply use tasks recorded by others and record their own tasks. On the other hand, inventive users who wish to exercise a greater degree of control over their desktops can dive right into ATL and begin creating scripts to carry out a range of activities.

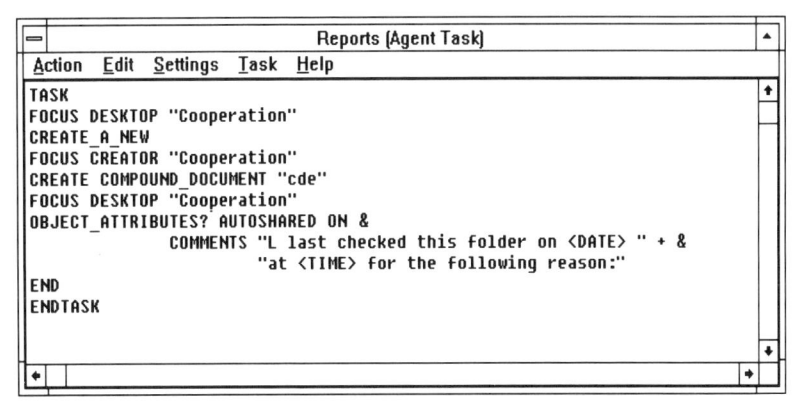

```
                         Reports (Agent Task)
 Action  Edit  Settings  Task  Help
TASK
FOCUS DESKTOP "Cooperation"
CREATE_A_NEW
FOCUS CREATOR "Cooperation"
CREATE COMPOUND_DOCUMENT "cde"
FOCUS DESKTOP "Cooperation"
OBJECT_ATTRIBUTES? AUTOSHARED ON &
             COMMENTS "L last checked this folder on <DATE> " + &
                     "at <TIME> for the following reason:"
END
ENDTASK
```

Figure 4-2: ATL Editor with Short Script

Each COOPERATION object type understands its own sub-set of ATL. For an object to be the recipient of an ATL command, it must have the "focus," a term that means it is the currently selected or active object. ATL has commands for setting and changing the focus to various objects as necessary in constructing a complex script. Typically, an ATL script opens an objects and then gives it the focus before sending it any commands.

ATL recognizes five data types:

- strings
- integers
- real numbers
- points
- regions (rectangular areas of the screen)

All tasks begin with the keyword TASK and end with the keyword ENDTASK. Between these two delimiters, ATL statements appear. Statements deal with opening and closing objects, setting the focus, and issuing commands to the currently focused object. Some commands require parameters; others can take optional parameters if appropriate. Outside the delimiters, an ATL script can include procedures that are called from various points within the script. Such procedures are quite similar to subroutines in conventional programming languages.

Here is a short ATL script fragment that empties the waste basket on the user's desktop. (The full script would include some error-checking and other activities that are not shown here.)

```
TASK
   FOCUS OFFICE
   IF Open_Waste# = 1
         OPEN
   ENDIF
   FOCUS WASTE_BASKET
   EMPTY
   IF Open_Waste# = 1
         CLOSE
   ENDIF
   END
ENDTASK
```

As you can see, this script sets the focus to the desktop (referred to as "OFFICE" here). The object with the focus is the object to which subsequent script instructions are sent. The script then opens the waste basket, empties it, and closes it again.

The Agent Task Language includes enough robustness to build miniapplications, complete with interface elements such as dialog boxes, warning sounds, and the like. It also includes the ability to use variables, functions, expressions, and control structures (loops and conditional processing operators). In other words, it is capable of producing a highly interactive and well-behaved interface to any task of arbitrary complexity that a user might want to perform in COOPERATION.

THE COOPERATION INTERFACE BUILDER

The ATL includes commands that let you construct simple interface elements such as pre-defined dialog boxes with simple "Yes" and "No" buttons in them. You can also program only slightly more complex dialog boxes with other buttons, but doing so requires you to know precisely where you want the buttons placed and other details you probably don't want to have to understand. Such dialogs are fine for things like confirming that the user really wants to throw away a particular object. But they aren't highly interactive and they allow the scripter or programmer no room for design creativity.

If the user interface to an agent task needs to be more polished looking or needs to permit the user to make several choices before executing a task, the COOPERATION Interface Builder is a more powerful tool.

The COOPERATION Interface Builder permits you to "draw" dialog boxes to be used in conjunction with agent tasks by simply picking a control type, clicking where you want it placed, providing basic information (such as names or labels), and connecting these interface components, as appropriate, to agent tasks. Figure 4-3 shows what the Interface Builder's main window looks like with one of each kind of control you can create in dialogs.

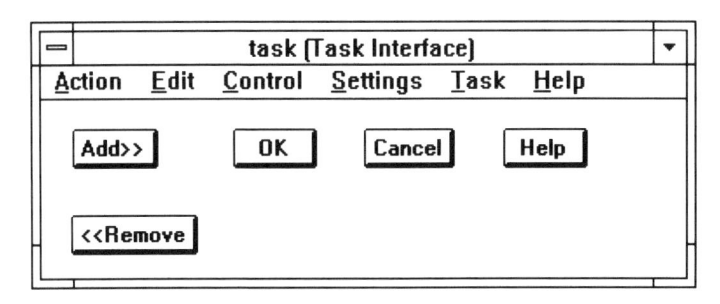

Figure 4-3: Interface Builder Main Window

A great deal of the pain and suffering usually involved in creating a user interface is eliminated in the COOPERATION Interface Builder. To add a control to the dialog, simply choose the type of control and click where you want it placed. You can always move it. Controls are automatically created at a pre-defined size, over which you have no real control. This limits your options somewhat but does ensure a standard look and feel for COOPERATION dialogs.

Figure 4-4 shows a complex dialog created using the COOPERATION Interface Builder. As you can see, you can create dialogs that look very much like those in major Windows and NewWave applications, including COOPERATION itself.

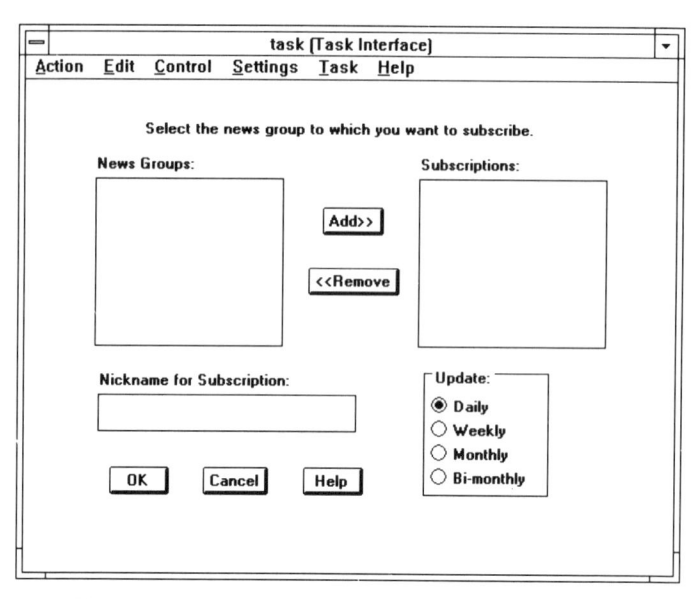

Figure 4-4: Sample Dialog Created with Interface Builder

Dialogs created with the Interface Builder can interact with tasks in two ways:

- an agent task can open an interface object
- an interface object can carry out agent tasks

Agents can open interface objects with ATL statements. Interface objects can initiate agent tasks either automatically (using a feature called "autostart") when the interface object is opened or in response to the user pressing a button. In most cases, the purpose of having the interface object involved in the task process dictates that we want the user to push a button to indicate that the information in the dialog is complete and accurate and that the task can proceed safely.

DESIGNING AND IMPLEMENTING AGENT TASKS

Many agent tasks that will be created by or for users will have little or no impact on the work group or the enterprise. It is likely that most COOPERATION agent tasks will be single-purpose, single-user activities to assist one person in the execution of a repetitive task. Such tasks obviously require less planning and design than tasks which will have a broader impact or be used by more people.

In this section, we will outline some suggestions for designing and implementing agent tasks in COOPERATION. Some of these suggestions are just common sense; they apply regardless of whether the task involved is one that only one user will ever see or one that everyone in the enterprise might use. Where we have specific suggestions that apply specifically to tasks with broader scope, we'll point that out.

The general process for designing and implementing tasks, then, is as follows:

1. Determine the scope of use of the finished task.
2. Define the problem being attacked.
3. Identify the COOPERATION objects involved in the solution.
4. Consider reusability if appropriate.
5. Determine the importance of the user interface, if any.
6. Write the script.
7. Test the script.

Let's look briefly at each of these steps.

DETERMINE SCOPE OF USE

Is the task to be used only the requestor? Or would other members of the work group find the task useful? Are there other work groups in the enterprise where the script might be welcomed?

The answers to these questions help shape the degree to which other steps in the design process become important. They also help decide how much complexity will be involved in reaching an acceptable design and an achievable schedule for completion of the task. Even a very small task can sometimes be quite useful throughout the enterprise if its function is sufficiently generic. On the other hand, involving too many possible users in the design process can slow things unnecessarily.

DEFINE THE PROBLEM

Any programming task—and scripting, no matter how trivial, is still programming on some levels—requires that the problem be sufficiently well defined that we can know when it's solved. With agent task scripts, this becomes even more important.

We really want to keep these tasks small and single-purpose. There are a number of reasons for this: simplicity, reusability, speed of execution, ease of modification and others. It is important, therefore, to break a proposed agent task into components that are as small as possible.

For example, if a user wants to have a task constructed that will log on to the company mainframe, check for electronic mail, download any messages, print them out, and archive them for later retrieval, it may well be a good idea to write several tasks rather than one complex task. Some of these tasks can be performed only by Communications Authoring Tool scripting, for example. Even if all of these activities were within the scope of ATL, however, it would still be a good idea to break the tasks into discrete components. Tasks can call other tasks stored in the same task project folder, so this kind of decomposition is efficient as well as effective.

Be sure, too, that if the task is going to be used by more than one work group in the enterprise, representatives of all involved groups are given an opportunity to respond to the problem statement. This may reveal holes in the localized view of one person.

IDENTIFY OBJECTS INVOLVED

What COOPERATION objects need to be involved in solving the problem we've just defined? Where do these objects reside? Do all of the people who wish to use the agent task when it's complete have appropriate access? If not, should their access be upgraded or should the objects be moved or should the task be re-analyzed?

Most tasks will involve only objects that are on the local workstation and on the work group server. But since COOPERATION deliberately masks from the user the issue of where objects reside, a user might ask for a script that would require far more enterprise-wide computing than it is possible or efficient to store in an agent task.

Since any object to be accessed by an agent task must be accessible to the workstation from which the task is run, this step is particularly important where multiple users and work groups are involved.

CONSIDER REUSABILITY

Scripts are not as reusable as objects, but they can be reused if they are designed well, remain special-purpose, and avoid "hard coding" things like user names, object names, and the like unless those elements really must be stored in the script.

This step is crucial if the task is to be shared. For example, if a payroll clerk wants an agent task script that will open a certain set of folders each morning and apprise him or her of the work to be done that day, this task script might be quite interesting to other payroll clerks. It may even be useful to people who are not payroll clerks. The clerk who asks for the task script (or even writes it) might call the primary folder "Incoming Tasks" while others might call it "Stuff to Do" or "Tasks." Such problems can be solved in one of two ways. Either we can impose a standard folder name on all users (not usually very popular) or we can write the task so that it asks the user—at least the first time it runs—to identify the folder to be checked.

DETERMINE THE IMPORTANCE OF THE UI

How important is it that the user interface have a polished look? How "user-proof" does it need to be in gathering information that could alter how it processes information?

In the case of a task script that will be used by one person or a small group of people with known characteristics, the user interface may be all but unimportant. Whether it feels and looks like other Windows or NewWave applications, for example, may be irrelevant to such people. Similarly, if most or all of a worker or work group's tasks are automated through agent tasks, and if this constitutes the bulk of their work in a given period, it may be perfectly acceptable to violate rules about user interface design.

But most agent scripts live in a real-world environment where users are accustomed to seeing certain kinds of elements in their Windows applications' user interfaces. To deviate significantly from these expectations is dangerous. That is not to say it should never be done, only that it should be done only for a clearly defined reason. It should also be a logical extension of the UI's rules so that users will find it comfortable even if not intuitive the first few times they use the interface.

Another part of the interface involves determining how the agent task will be initiated by the user. It can be attached to a menu or connected to a user interface. It can also simply be stored on the desktop, waiting for the user to drop it onto the Agent tool. The on-line help available for the design of agents has some helpful information on these points.

WRITE THE SCRIPT

Once we now what problem we're trying to solve, who is going to use the script, how modular it needs to be, and how it will interact with the user, we can just sit down and write the script. Scripts typically take far less time to write than full-fledged programs, but this doesn't mean they are all trivial and require only a couple of hours' work. On the contrary, some collections of scripts with which the authors are familiar occupy thousands of lines of scripting code and took weeks or even a few months to complete.

But most scripts are relatively simple and quite small. They can usually be written in a day or two, often in an hour or less.

TEST THE SCRIPT

Testing involves not only determining if the script works when all goes well, but what happens when unexpected events arise. For example, what does the script do if it tries to set the focus on an object that the user has deleted or moved? What if the server is not available when the agent asks for a file stored there?

There is another level of testing to be done if the script is to be used by more than one person. Be sure to test the script thoroughly both on the creator's system and on at least one other system. This will uncover hard-coded assumptions about the names of objects, their locations, user names, and so forth.

What kinds of things can and should you test for in your ATL scripts? There are two kinds of things that can go wrong with a script when it is being run: data entry errors that cause unexpected results and logic errors.

To test for the first kind of errors, when you are running the script and testing it, try entering inappropriate data and see how the script behaves. For example, if you are asking the user how many copies of a document to send to the mail system and the user says "Five" or "Aunt Nell," what does the script do? You may want to add some statements to the script to check for such erroneous data and behave gracefully when the user makes a mistake.

Logic errors are harder to find and test for, but you need to think about them. As a rule, they reveal themselves quickly, but sometimes they can be quite insidious and "hide" for days! The most common logic errors occur in the use of variables and conditional logic. For example, you might assign a value to the variable NUMOBJ in one place to indicate how many objects are involved in a process. Later in the same script, you might use NUMOBJ to mean the identifying number of the current object. This can result in some difficult problems. Or you might want to check a file to see if it is either a contract or a personnel requisition but if you used AND logic instead of OR logic, you'd never find any documents because there aren't any contracts that are also personnel requisitions.

PART TWO:
Maximizing COOPERATION®

5
Getting Started with COOPERATION

This chapter introduces and explains the steps involved in getting started with COOPERATION in your organization. It begins with a discussion of why a gradual implementation will facilitate the phased introduction of COOPERATION into your company. It also explains how to undertake a phasesd implementation and describes the installation process from an overview perspective, defining the roles played by you and by NCR staff.

If you already have COOPERATION installed and running, feel free to skip this chapter.

The four major steps in assembling the required resources to enable your COOPERATION installation are the subject of the subsequent section of this chapter. The chapter concludes by describing the prerequisites for installing and using COOPERATION: what hardware is required and what experience various people involved in the installation should have.

IMPLEMENTING COOPERATION IN PHASES

Because COOPERATION encourages people to re-examine and often change the way they work with their computer systems, you should implement it in phases rather than converting your entire organization at one time. In this section, we will discuss additional reasons for taking this approach and suggest two primary methods for achieving phased implementation of COOPERATION.

WHY DEPLOY IN PHASES?

Sometimes we are so eager to adopt a new technology that we want to jump right into its use without spending much time in analysis and planning. It is one thing to indulge this tendency when the change affects only you and your way of working (for example, when you buy the latest shrink-wrapped desktop presentation program). However, when many people are affected, it is important to sequence the adoption process in a way that allows the people involved in the change-over to absorb it. When you are moving from a traditional computer system to one that fosters a higher degree of interaction among group members, this point is even more significant.

There are additional reasons for a phased deployment of enterprise-level systems like COOPERATION. Here are some of the most important.

- It is important that all members of a group feel involved in the process of choosing and deploying the new system with which they are going to. If you stage the implementation of COOPERATION, you will increase staff members' feelings of personal involvement.

- Training in the use of a new system like COOPERATION is an important part of the installation. If you try to deploy the system throughout the organization all at once, you will find yourself, of necessity, trying to pass on more information than people can absorb in a short time frame. The result may be frustration with the system and a reluctance to use it.
- Organizational work must still get done during the transition. Switching from your present system to COOPERATION in stages permits you to continue to work at your former degree of efficiency while you move to the new system.

HOW TO APPROACH IMPLEMENTING COOPERATION

Figure 5-1 depicts the two primary approaches to a phased implementation of any enterprise-level system, including COOPERATION.

DIVIDE AND CONQUER   **UNITE AND CONQUER**

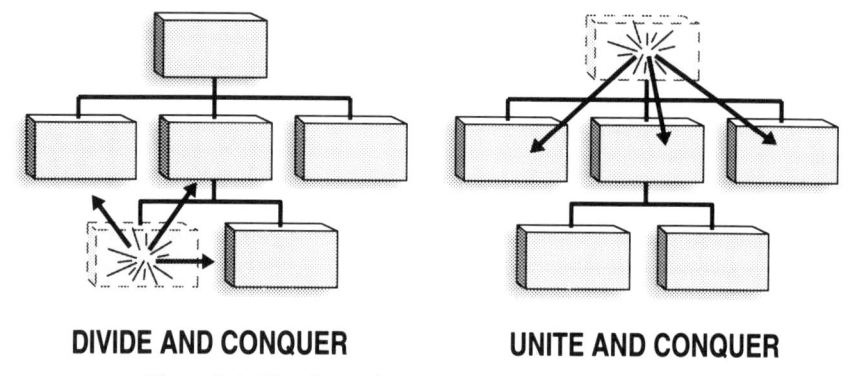

Figure 5-1: Two Strategies for Introducing COOPERATION

The *divide-and-conquer* strategy calls for you to implement COOPERATION in a department or a sub-set of departments initially and then roll it out through the rest of the organization. As soon as one department has implemented the new system, other departments have more reasons to adopt the new system. For one thing, they will see the other department's success and want to participate. For another, sharing information among departments becomes increasingly important as the advantages of electronic COOPERATION become apparent to the organization.

On the other hand, the *unite-and-conquer* strategy involves deploying the new system at the top level of an organization and then rolling it down to subordinate groups. This approach has two advantages over the divide-and-conquer strategy. First, it provides the much-needed top-management support required to facilitate the move to the new system. The whole issue of deployment of the system is seen from the beginning as an enterprise-wide concern, crossing departmental and work-group boundaries.

Second, top management gets the benefit of the system's information-gathering and decision support facilities early in the process. Since this level is where the big-picture decisions in the organization are made, the power of COOPERATION is clear much sooner than with the divide-and-conquer strategy. In addition, top management's need for information drives the subordinate organizations to implement COOPERATION quickly to stay in touch with the needs and wishes of top management.

Of course, these two strategies are not mutually exclusive. In fact, most companies use them in combination, rolling COOPERATION out across departments while also constructiong a top-down, executive-level system for tying the departments together.

WHO'S RESPONSIBLE FOR WHAT?

The process of installing and deploying NCR's COOPERATION environment in your enterprise can be viewed from the top level as looking something like Figure 5-2.

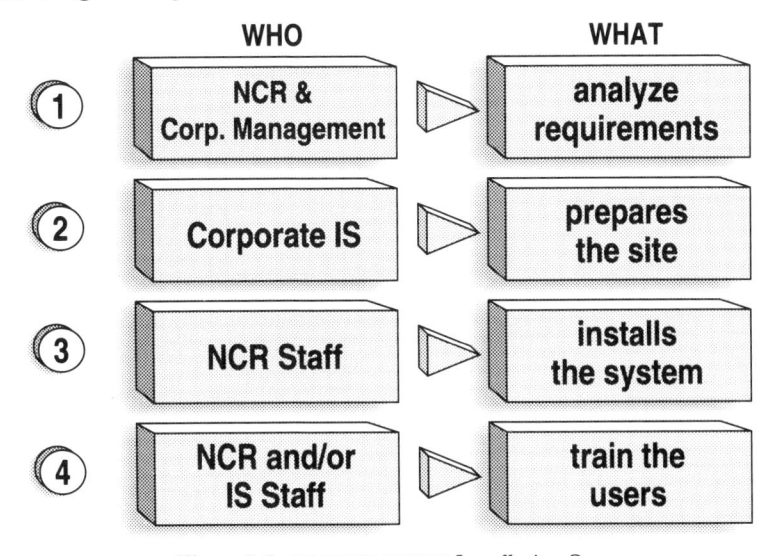

WHO	WHAT
① NCR & Corp. Management	analyze requirements
② Corporate IS	prepares the site
③ NCR Staff	installs the system
④ NCR and/or IS Staff	train the users

Figure 5-2: COOPERATION Installation Sequence

As you can see, the installation process is not something you will undertake alone. Each COOPERATION customer is assigned a team from NCR to assist in each phase of the design and implementation of the system.

First, you will analyze your enterprise's requirements. In this step, you will define exactly what you want to accomplish with COOPERATION, including activities that you may or may not be doing at the moment. You'll also identify the legacy systems you wish to bring along to the new world of COOPERATION. (Legacy systems are existing applications and databases that you need to continue to use even as you move to a COOPERATION-based environment.) At this stage, you need to ensure that your IS department personnel are receiving appropriate training in COOPERATION and its installation and support.

Site preparation includes ensuring that the proper hardware is available, that appropriately trained personnel are on hand to assist in the process, and that your facilities are adequate to support COOPERATION.

When the site is ready, NCR will handle the installation of COOPERATION. Corporate IS personnel may be required to provide support at various points in the process, but the primary task of installation falls to NCR.

Once the system is installed, it is important that you undertake three types of training:

- End users must be taught to use the tools and desktops that have been designed and installed specifically to enable your enterprise to accomplish its objectives.

- Management personnel must be educated in how COOPERATION can and should change the way they and their staffs work and communicate.

- Administrators must be taught how to configure and maintain the system.

ASSEMBLING THE REQUIRED RESOURCES

Four types of resources are needed to carry out a successful installation of COOPERATION, as shown in Figure 5-3.

In conjunction with an NCR representative, you will determine which of the many components that make up a fully configured COOPERATION environment are best suited to your company's specific needs. You may define some elements that you want to put into place in the future but which need not be part of the initial installation.

Once you know how big a system installation you will be undertaking, you can recruit and assign adoption roles to appropriate people. We will have more to say about that a little later in this chapter when we look at the people needed for the COOPERATION installation team.

One of COOPERATION's real strengths is that it doesn't require you to abandon your established software or to undergo a series of time-consuming

```
    COOPERATION                    trained
    components                      staff




      hardware                    legacy
      platform                    systems
```

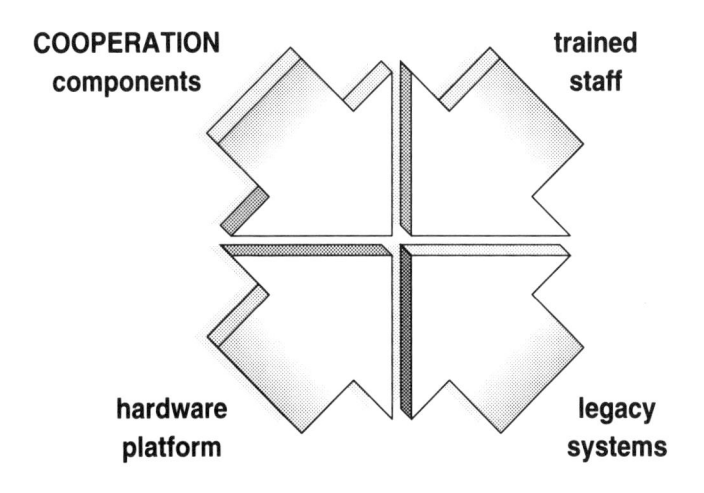

Figure 5-3: Key Requirements for Installing COOPERATION

and cumbersome file conversion processes. Your legacy systems fit right into the COOPERATION system. Defining which of your legacy systems should be incorporated into COOPERATION and which should be replaced by COOPERATION's own components is important. Before you can do that, you need a careful inventory and analysis of your existing systems.

BEFORE YOU INSTALL COOPERATION

The process of planning and gearing up for the implementation of COOPERATION is covered in detail in the *COOPERATION Planning Guide*, available from NCR, but we will look briefly at two of the most important issues involved here: hardware requirements and the experience level of the people involved in the project.

WHAT HARDWARE IS NEEDED?

By its nature, COOPERATION is a network-based product. When you think about the hardware required to support a COOPERATION installation, you must therefore think about the server and the workstations that will make up the network.

The server is where the bulk of the COOPERATION software is stored. It acts as the hub of the network to which the workstations are attached. If you have a local area network (LAN) established in your enterprise, you probably have most of the hardware you need for a COOPERATION server. You can use multiple servers with COOPERATION as well. In that case, one server is identified as the "Installation Server."

To support COOPERATION, a server must meet the following requirements:

- 80386 or 80486-based Micro Channel Architecture (MCA)
- sufficient slots to hold LAN card, SCSI adapter, communications card, bus mouse if used and any memory expansion required
- NCR OS/2, current version
- hard disk drive with sufficient storage
- at least one 3.5-inch, 1.44MB floppy disk drive
- VGA display
- NCR-supplied SCSI tape device
- CD-ROM for at least one server in each domain
- Token Ring or Ethernet LAN with NCR-supported interface boards
- a supported printer

A COOPERATION workstation must meet the following requirements:

- 80386/80486 systems (NCR PC386 or PC486 or equivalent)
- hard disk
- VGA display
- floppy disk drive (3.5-inch, 1.44 MB or 5.25-inch 1.2 MB)

The preceding requirements are for an OS/2 installation.

By the time you read this, UNIX support may well be available as well.

WHAT EXPERIENCE IS REQUIRED FROM YOUR PEOPLE?

At a minimum, you will want to build a team of people that includes a project manager, an architecture consultant, a non-technical system administrator, and one or more technical system administrators, depending on such factors as:

- how many components of COOPERATION you are installing
- how many organizational elements are involved in the installation
- what network and other site-specific installation problems exist

In a large COOPERATION project, it would not be unusual for the team responsible for the installation, operation, and maintenance of the system to involve a dozen or more people. The general structure of this team is shown in Figure 5-4.

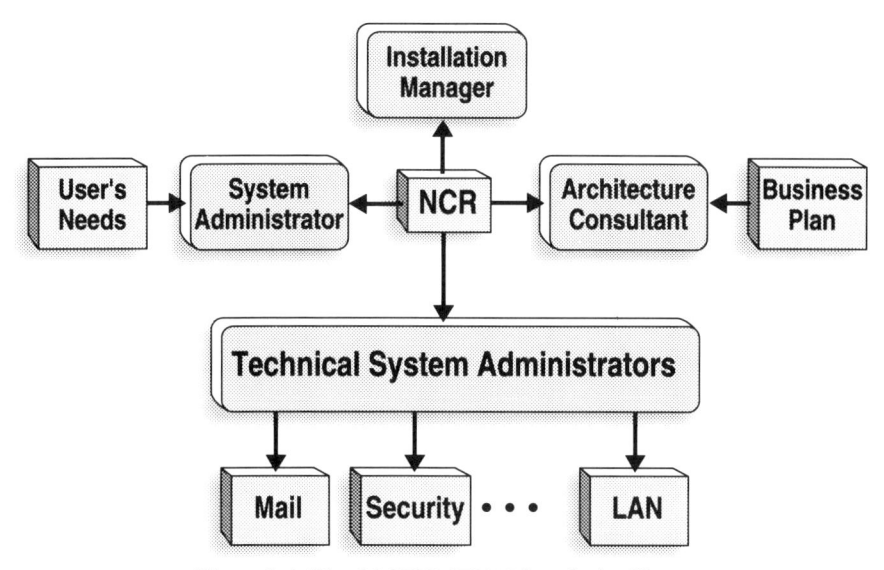

Figure 5-4: The COOPERATION Installation Team

The person chosen to manage the installation of COOPERATION should have a good background in project management and in object-oriented technology. This person will be responsible for ensuring that the project stays on schedule and that the final project's acceptance criteria are well thought-out and met.

The architecture consultant on the COOPERATION project should be someone with a good grounding in DOS, data communications and OS/2. This person should also have a background in information engineering. As the project develops, the architect is responsible for translating your enterprise's strategic business information plan into a viable and effective COOPERATION design. Before beginning this assignment, this person should become comfortable with the architecture and functionality of COOPERATION.

Non-technical system administrators act as the interface between the technical staff and end users. They assist end users in resolving operational problems, work with the help desk to resolve problems and coordinate end user training. During the planning and installation of the COOPERATION system, non-technical system administrators review the design with the end user in mind and suggest changes as appropriate. This person needs no specific technical background but does require a basic understanding of how COOPERATION works. This background can be obtained from NCR documentation and on-line tutorials.

Technical System Administrators typically operate at the enterprise level of the organization. You may wish to have one or more such individuals responsible for understanding the technical nuances of COOPERATION Mail, Information Storage Manager, security, Archive and Restore, the Supply Cabinet and network connections. Individuals assigned to these tasks should have a good understanding of DOS and OS/2. They should also be well-grounded in all of COOPERATION's basic modules, including the end user's perspective. These people serve as resources to the non-technical system administrator, who typically works at the department or work group level.

6
The Application Environment

COOPERATION includes several applications that will make your work more efficient and effective the moment you begin using the environment. It also provides a complete set of tools and application frameworks for constructing your own applications. Both of these aspects of COOPERATION are constantly expanding. The information in this book describes the application elements of COOPERATION in the first release of the product. By the time you begin to explore COOPERATION, you will probably find much more awaiting you.

This chapter begins with a section that describes COOPERATION's built-in applications. That section opens with an introduction to the COOPERATION Group Calendar application. It then discusses the Business Information Monitor (BIM), a tool set you will find yourself using more and more as you learn what it can do for you. Next, it describes the use and role of compound document editing. Then it provides a brief discussion of Mail, Remote Application Access (RAA) and the related Communications Authoring Tool (CAT) applications.

The second section of this chapter is devoted to the tools COOPERATION includes for adding other applications to the environment. It talks about how to incorporate existing, shrink-wrapped DOS and Windows applications. It then explains how your organization can use its own resources to create new applications for use in COOPERATION.

At the close of this chapter, we discuss the kinds of applications you can expect NCR to provide in future releases of COOPERATION.

COOPERATION'S BUILT-IN APPLICATIONS

COOPERATION is delivered with a number of business applications that enable you to become more efficient at your daily tasks regardless of what other DOS or Windows applications you might use for day-to-day activities.

GROUP CALENDAR
Group Calendar is actually a single name for a collection of calendars that you will find useful in managing time, keeping track of appointments and to-do lists, and other time-related tasks. There are three types of calendars in this application as shown in Figure 6-1.

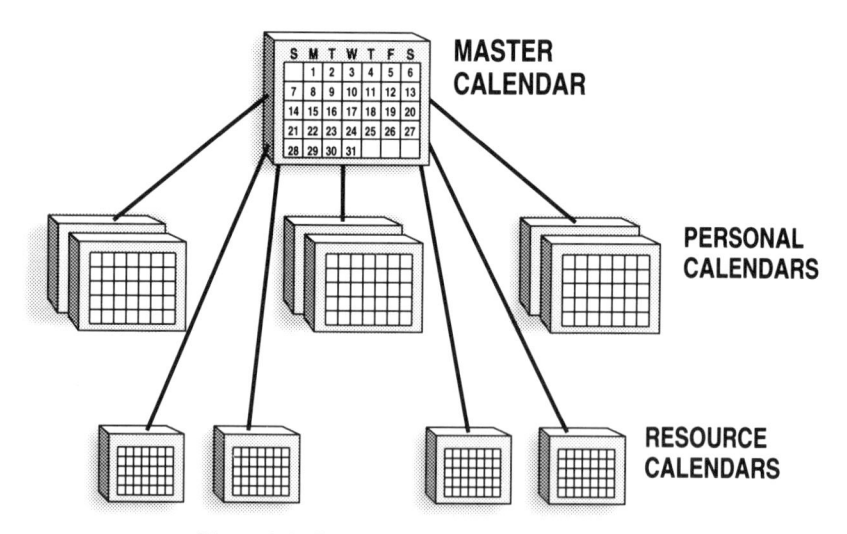

Figure 6-1: Components of The Group Calendar

All three calendars look and behave substantially similarly to one another so that learning how to use any calendar leads to rapid understanding of any other calendar in COOPERATION. For example, all calendars can be viewed by day, week, month, or year, and moving between views is handled identically in all calendars.

The Master Calendar is shared by all members of a work group. Each user has an icon to access the Master Calendar. Both the icon and the central Master Calendar are automatically created as part of the COOPERATION installation process. The Master Calendar is the central repository of individual work group members' schedules. If you want to schedule a meeting with some or all of the people in your work group, for example, you would use the Master Calendar to check everyone's availability.

In fact, scheduling meetings is such a common activity that the Master Calendar has built-in routines to handle all of the requisite processing. Any member of the work group can schedule a meeting by opening the Master Calendar and choosing "Schedule Meeting..." from the "Entries" menu. The ensuing dialog (Figure 6-2) lets the user describe the meeting, choose attendees and invitees, set up the date-time range for the meeting, and then schedule it.

The Master Calendar is connected to individual calendars as well, so the person trying to schedule a meeting can use the "Find Time..." button to find an open slot for all of the people who are to be asked to attend the

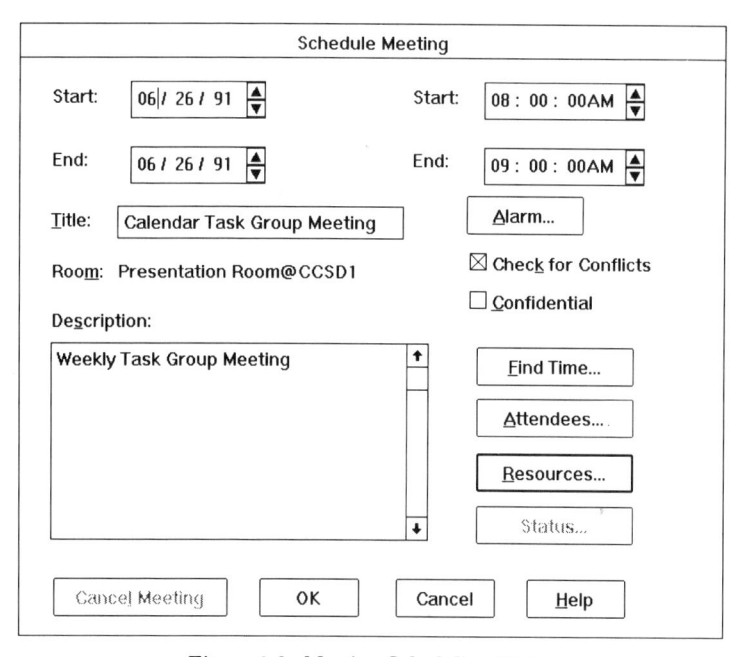

Figure 6-2: Meeting Scheduling Dialog

meeting. If a user attempts to schedule a meeting and one or more attendees have a conflict, COOPERATION informs the user that the meeting could not be scheduled. Once a meeting is successfully scheduled, COOPERATION automatically sends mail messages to all of the attendees.

Users can create as many individual calendars as they like. Many COOPERATION users create a general calendar to keep track of miscellaneous and personal-time activities and a specialized calendars for each project or task force with which they are involved. Individual calendars, like the Master Calendar, permit users to store appointments, To Do items and reminders.

- Appointments are scheduled activities that always relate to dates and times.

- To Do items have no connections to time. They are carried over automatically from day to day until they are marked complete or deleted by the user.

- Reminders are similar to To Do items but do not carry forward if not disposed of on the day they are entered.

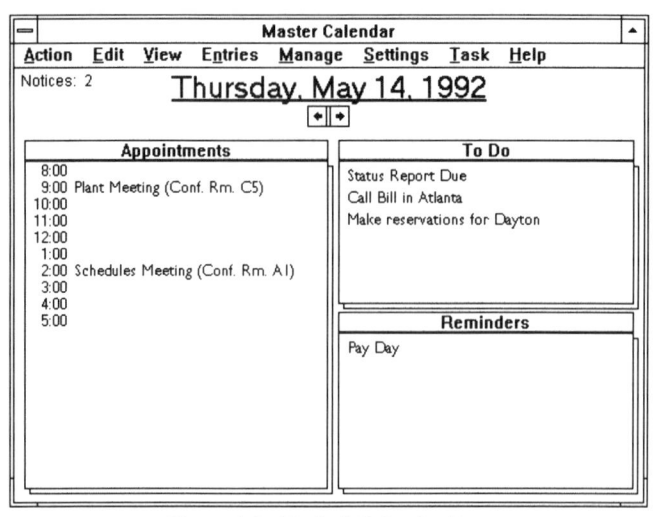

```
┌─────────────────────────────────────────────────────────────┐
│ ═ │              Master Calendar                      │ ▲ │
│ Action  Edit  View  Entries  Manage  Settings  Task  Help   │
│ Notices: 2      Thursday, May 14, 1992                      │
│                      ◆ ◆                                     │
│ ┌───────Appointments─────────┬──────────To Do────────────┐  │
│ │ 8:00                       │ Status Report Due         │  │
│ │ 9:00 Plant Meeting (Conf. Rm. C5) │ Call Bill in Atlanta      │  │
│ │ 10:00                      │ Make reservations for Dayton │  │
│ │ 11:00                      │                           │  │
│ │ 12:00                      │                           │  │
│ │ 1:00                       │                           │  │
│ │ 2:00 Schedules Meeting (Conf. Rm. A1) ├──────Reminders────────────┤  │
│ │ 3:00                       │                           │  │
│ │ 4:00                       │ Pay Day                   │  │
│ │ 5:00                       │                           │  │
│ └────────────────────────────┴───────────────────────────┘  │
└─────────────────────────────────────────────────────────────┘
```

Figure 6-3: Typical Calendar Page

Figure 6-3 shows a typical calendar page with appointments, To Do items and reminders entered.

The third type of COOPERATION calendar is a resource calendar. Resource calendars are used to schedule access to resources such as meeting and conference rooms, audio-visual equipment, and company cars. They are typically owned and managed by the person in the organization responsible for the management of the resource, though they can be shared so that others can schedule their use without bothering the resource manager. Resource calendars can be tied to the Master Calendar so that users trying to schedule a meeting can locate an appropriate facility that is available.

Both user and resource calendars can be configured so that items entered into them are automatically registered in the appropriate Master Calendar. This permits anyone who accesses the Master Calendar to see all appointments other than those the user marks as "Confidential."

BUSINESS INFORMATION MONITOR

A Business Information Monitor (BIM) is a mechanism by which users can keep track of key business indicators and activities and be warned when something in the business requires attention. We can look at the BIM aspects of COOPERATION from two viewpoints: that of the user and that of the builder. We'll look first from the user's perspective.

The User's View of BIM

A BIM object (see Figure 6-4) appears on your desktop for any monitor installed on it. Each such object consists of one or more views, which may in turn be related to one another in a tree (see Figure 6-5).

Figure 6-4: Icon for a BIM Object

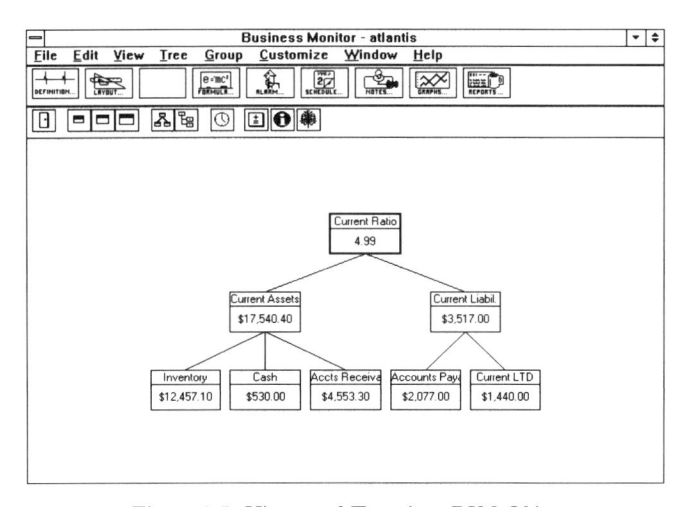

Figure 6-5: Views and Trees in a BIM Object

A view is the most basic unit of information in BIM. There are two types of views: query views, which retrieve information from databases and/or spreadsheets and display the result; and formula views, which manipulate the information retrieved by query views or other formula views. BIM objects make extensive use of data stored in spreadsheets and database files. BIM is not, however, a spreadsheet or database program object. Instead, it draws information from these objects to monitor business activities.

The most useful property of a view from the user's perspective is its alarm status. This status can be any of the following: normal, caution, or alert. Each of these can be associated with a color in BIM; typically, normal is shown by a green signal, caution by yellow and alert by red. This permits the user to see at a glance if any of the business measures or activities being monitored requires immediate attention.

BIM objects are nested so that the user can "drill down" to a level of detail sufficient to determine the cause of an alarm. The user can open a tree, select a view to examine, and then open it to greater levels of detail until the cause of the problem is revealed.

Information trees are arranged so that parent views appear above child views in the hierarchy. Child views provide information to the parent view. which may in turn perform some calculations to determine the alarm status of the BIM object.

BIM objects can display their information in the form of reports, graphs, simple numbers, or various other ways, depending on the use to which the builder anticipated they would be put.

The Builder's View of BIM

A BIM builder is a person who creates new BIM objects and manages the BIM environment, including passwords.

To build a BIM object or to modify an existing one, the user must have been granted an appropriate level of access to BIM. Such a user can then carry out all of the following functions with regard to BIM objects, using dialogs and built-in list managers to minimize the amount of typing that must be done to build a useful BIM object:

- define a view's type, source of data, and other options
- select the database or file containing the data for the view if it uses an external data file
- formulate a SQL query to obtain data from a database or other SQL source if appropriate
- create a formula to carry out a calculation
- link the view to other Windows applications via Dynamic Data Exchange (DDE) if that is chosen as the source of data for the view
- set alarm ranges and conditions for the view
- schedule the time interval between recalculations of the view
- attach notes to the view
- design and attach one or more graphs to a view and choose the type of graph, color scheme to be used, size of graph, variables to be graphed, and other details
- design and create a report for the view

As you can see, most of these operations are concerned with the source of the data being monitored by a view or used by a view to carry out a calculation to pass on to another view. Information can be stored in any popular database or spreadsheet file, stored on the local machine, on the LAN or even remotely. You can also define the type of data to be displayed by the view, including most of the standard spreadsheet data types and formats.

BIM builders also have control over the passwords that are required to gain various levels of access to a BIM object. Such objects have three types of access, as do most COOPERATION objects:

- owner
- builder
- user

Different passwords can be associated with each of these levels of access. In fact, multiple passwords can be defined by the BIM builder for each type of access.

COMPOUND DOCUMENT EDITING

Modern-day business needs call for the ability to create and use documents that incorporate many types of data: text, graphs, spreadsheet segments, drawings, tables, annotations, and even sound and video notes. COOPERATION supports this notion of compound document editing in two ways.

- In its early release, COOPERATION includes an application called the Compound Document Editor, or CDE. This application is a full-featured word processor that also handles compound documents.

- As it matures, COOPERATION will enable users to incorporate their own choice of a compound document editor such as Lotus' Ami Pro and other, similar applications.

The remainder of this section describes the capabilities of the built-in CDE program that is part of COOPERATION's initial release.

Compound documents in COOPERATION can contain data such as text, spreadsheets, and TIFF (Tagged Image File Format) graphics. In addition to those currently supported, NCR plans to add more data types in subsequent releases (see "Coming Attractions," below). Used in conjunction with the text conversion facility of COOPERATION, discussed in Chapter 7, the Compound Document Editor permits users to create, store, manipulate, share, mail, and otherwise manage documents of arbitrary complexity within a single editing environment.

As shown in Figure 6-6, the user can simply drag non-text objects into a compound document, position and size them, and they are thereby incorporated. Text can be readily entered into compound documents without the need to create a separate text object outside the editor and drag it in. Objects moved into a compound document are linked to the source document or application with "hot links." This means that if the data in the source changes while the compound document is open, the compound document will be automatically updated.

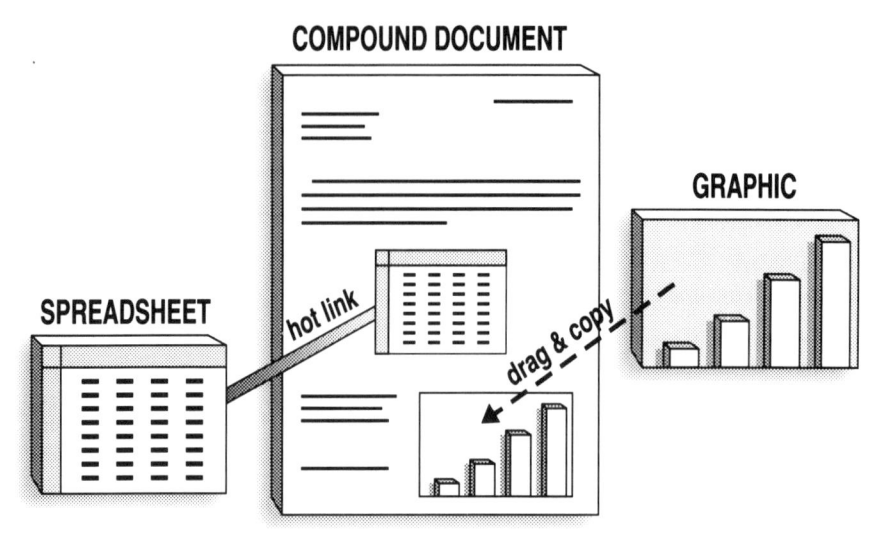

Figure 6-6: Creating Compound Documents

Users will find the Compound Document Editor helpful as they gain experience with it and create new masters in the form of document templates that provide a starting point object with which to create newsletters, memos, various kinds of letters, meeting notes, and other documents they need to create frequently.

In addition to the creation of such compound documents, the editor also provides support for the following functions:

- bookmarks, by which users can move around in the document and recall important or interesting contents later without having to remember where things are located

- a dictionary tool that permits the user to check the spelling in a document

ELECTRONIC MAIL AND COMMUNICATIONS APPLICATIONS

Because it is intended to be used primarily in networked work group environments, COOPERATION includes a number of functions to support communication among users and between users and the server. We'll take a brief look at some of these facilities in this section, in the following order:

- electronic mail
- remote application access (RAA)
- Communications Authoring Tool (CAT)

COOPERATION Mail

As you would probably expect from an object-oriented mail system, COOPERATION Mail permits users to transfer even complex objects throughout the COOPERATION system. Objects need not be "disassembled" into their component parts and mailed separately; they can be sent over the network via electronic mail as if they were single items containing but a single type of data.

The user's interaction with COOPERATION Mail happens on two levels. On the explicit, conscious level, the user has on the desktop an Out Tray, where outgoing mail may be placed, an In Tray, where incoming mail appears, and one or more Address Books that permit the creation and management of custom distribution lists. In addition to these tools, the user also works with objects such as envelopes, distribution lists, and phone messages. On a transparent level, users will often receive mail from and send mail to other users without explicitly placing anything in their Out Tray. The Group Calendar's meeting scheduling system, described earlier in this chapter, is an example of such transparent mail use.

COOPERATION Mail is compatible, via mail gateways, with most popular electronic mail systems, including IBM PROFS, HPDesk, Wang OFFICE, and Novell's MHS. Ultimately, mail transfer is handled by the Post Office, an application on the COOPERATION server. The architecture of the Mail facility is shown in Figure 6-7.

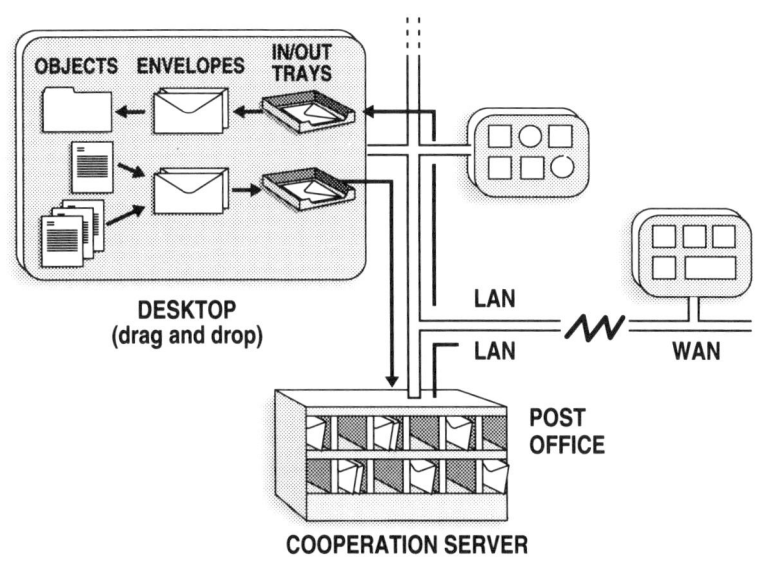

Figure 6-7: Architecture of COOPERATION Mail

Users mail objects to other COOPERATION users by dragging them to the Out Tray or by placing several objects in an envelope and then dragging the envelope to the Out Tray. Mail users can control a number of aspects of the mail system's operation on their desktops, including sharing it with other users, automatically forwarding mail to another workstation, how they are to be notified when mail arrives in their In Tray, and a number of other such properties of the system.

The COOPERATION Mail system is completely scriptable via Desktop Agent Task Language operations described in Chapter 4.

Remote Application Access

Remote Application Access: provides users with an easy way to construct, store, and execute remote log-in procedures to systems located throughout the enterprise and to retrieve information from those systems to their desktops.

RAA supports a wide range of terminal emulations, data transfer protocols, and communications methodologies so that it fits as neatly as possible into existing telecommunications facilities. Users interact with the remote systems via terminal emulation windows and edit windows. Each COOPERATION workstation can have up to four concurrent telecommunications sessions active at once. These four can be any combination of synchronous and asynchronous links that requires four or fewer sessions. Users can copy and paste information from these session windows to other COOPERATION objects, notably compound documents. Figure 6-8 shows an example of how RAA might be configured.

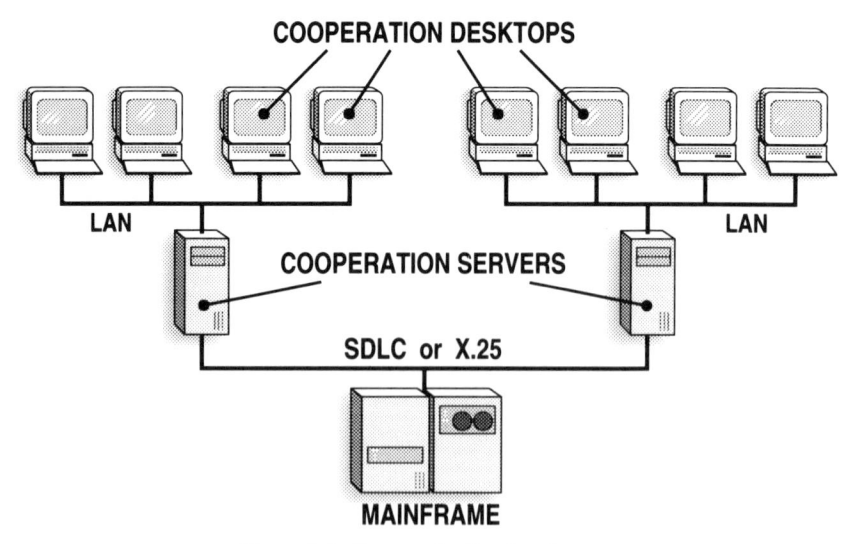

Figure 6-8: Remote Application Access

Editing windows are used to write scripts in the Communications Authoring Tool (CAT), which we will discuss in the next section.

Terminal emulation under RAA requires various gateway and protocol software from the COOPERATION suite, depending on the type of network configuration, telecommunications needs, and other variables.

Communications Authoring Tool

The Communications Authoring Tool (CAT) is an extension of Remote Application Access (RAA). Scripts designed to run in RAA and control terminal sessions are written using the CAT.

Besides telecommunications sessions, CAT scripts can be used to control Windows programs through their Dynamic Data Exchange (DDE) interfaces.

RAA scripts written with the CAT can retrieve, view, and manipulate information during multiple on-line sessions. Users can run scripts that extract text from one or more local or remote application windows and put the information into the CAT viewing window. These scripts can log the user onto the appropriate remote host, locate the desired database, search and retrieve the requested data, disconnect from the host, and return the data to the calling user's desktop.

Creation of CAT scripts is generally the province of an advanced user, who is defined as someone who has some knowledge of data transfer/ exchange and communications procedures and methods. This user must also understand how the applications that use the data will expect to find and use the information being retrieved. To support them in this effort, the CAT includes a Graphical Script Editor (see Figure 6-9).

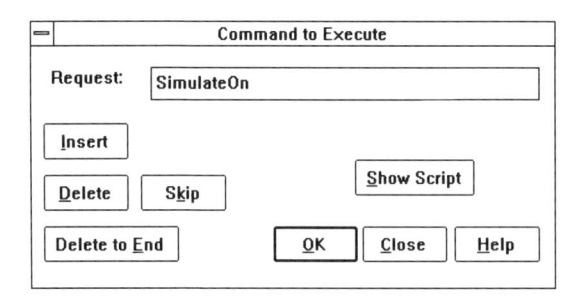

Figure 6-9: Graphical Script Editor in CAT

Through this Graphical Script Editor, the user can place the CAT Control Window into "Teach" mode. The system then watches the user's actions and records them in much the same way as desktop agent and menu tasks can be developed. The scripter can also "hot link" segments of text in two or more windows so that changes in one window are automatically reflected in the others. This environment also incorporates a full-powered script editor and a script executor for testing.

Coming Attractions

NCR plans to continue to enhance and extend the power of COOPERATION. Because it is built in such a strongly object-oriented manner, COOPERATION lends itself to such extensions more easily than conventional business computer systems .

If the version of COOPERATION with which you are working does not yet incorporate full work-flow automation, you should expect to see that capability added in the very near future. Also planned for future releases of the product as this book went to press were the following features:

- image scanning, storage, retrieval, and reproduction in compound documents
- optical character recognition (OCR)
- document annotation via "electronic post-it notes"
- full FAX server support
- HyperForm, for creating intelligent on-line forms

USING OTHER APPLICATIONS WITH COOPERATION

COOPERATION is an open environment to which new applications can be easily added (see Figure 6-10). In this section, we will look at the general processes involved in adding DOS legacy applications, Windows applications, and newly developed applications into the COOPERATION world.

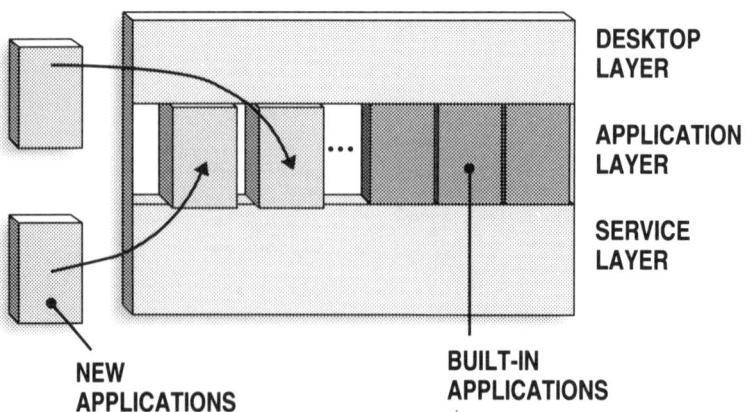

Figure 6-10: Adding New Applications

BRIDGES TO THE WORLD OF MS-DOS

Like any other Microsoft Windows-based application, COOPERATION permits you to open MS-DOS applications through the Windows Program Manager. But once users get accustomed to the concept of creating objects rather than opening documents and launching applications, it is both difficult and counter-productive to expect them to return to the old way of doing things.

To enable you to integrate MS-DOS applications more fully and seamlessly into the COOPERATION environment, the notion of bridges was developed. A DOS bridge is a vehicle that permits you to add MS-DOS applications and their primary document types to the list of things COOPERATION users can create by choosing "Create A New..." from the "Objects" menu.

Dozens of pre-built bridges are available from many sources and a large number are shipped with COOPERATION. Creating new ones is not difficult, although it is a task that should be reserved for someone with a basic understanding of COOPERATION and of the MS-DOS application(s) to be bridged.

Creating a new bridge begins the same way as creating any other type of COOPERATION object: by choosing "Create a New..." from the "Objects" menu. Choose the "Bridge Builder" object from the resulting dialog, give it a name, and then double-click it from the COOPERATION desktop. You will be presented with a window (see Figure 6-11) from which you can create a new bridge object.

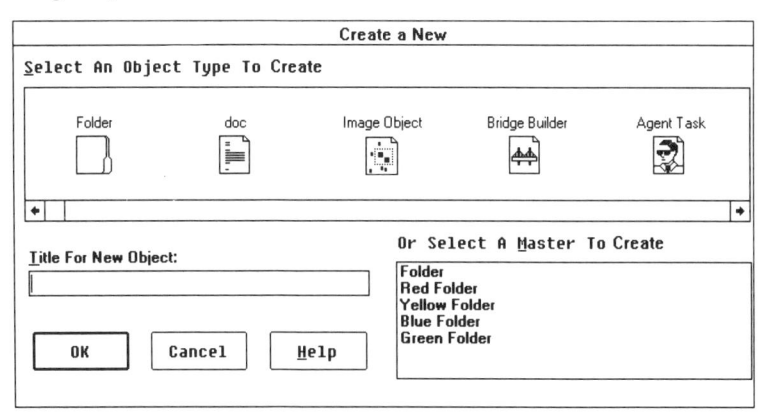

Figure 6-11: Bridge–Building Window

You can provide a minimal amount of information about an MS-DOS application, but the more information you can supply, the more tightly the application and its documents will be integrated into the COOPERATION desktop. In fact, it is possible for advanced programmers to create entirely new bridges to MS-DOS applications that bind them into the COOPERATION environment so tightly that they are indistinguishable from objects built into COOPERATION when it is installed.

Once an application has been bridged into COOPERATION, users create new documents with those applications in exactly the same way as they do with built-in object types. They can also create master template objects where they are appropriate and supported by the original application.

Users can import Bridge objects from disk with the "Import from File..." option on the "Objects" menu. They can also export such objects. This makes it possible for users to control the number of bridge objects from which they have to choose when they create a new object in COOPERATION. Bridges, like all other COOPERATION objects, can also be mailed between users.

INTEGRATING WINDOWS APPLICATIONS

Bridges much like those used for MS-DOS applications (see previous section) can also be built for Windows-compatible applications. The process is identical. There are also dozens of pre-built bridges available from various electronic bulletin boards and user groups to supplement those that are shipped with COOPERATION. Before constructing a new bridge, you should check the availability of a pre-built bridge for the application.

Applications which are NewWave-compatible or NewWave-aware can be integrated into COOPERATION much more easily and directly. This type of application is simply imported to the user's desktop. Thereafter, the "Create a New..." option on the "Objects" menu will reflect the ability to create new instances of such objects.

BUILDING NEW COOPERATION APPLICATIONS

COOPERATION provides an extensive array of programming interfaces through which new applications can be built on existing COOPERATION functionality.

These interfaces come in two forms:

1. APIs: Application Programming interfaces allow programmers to add new functions using the C language.

2. OPIs: Object Programming Interfaces provide complete access to the class structures built into COOPERATION using the C++ language.

Of the two alternatives, OPIs are much more powerful because they allow programmers to add classes to the existing COOPERATION class library, subclass existing classes, and take full advantage of the object–oriented basis of the product.

WHAT'S IN STORE FOR COOPERATION DEVELOPMENT?

In future releases, NCR will support object-oriented development environments such as C++ and Smalltalk so that programmers who wish to build extensions to or applications to work with COOPERATION can do so using object-oriented programming strategies.

Meanwhile, as we indicated earlier, NCR itself will continue to extend and enhance the power of COOPERATION and its applications in subsequent releases.

7
COOPERATION Services

As we saw in Chapters 3 and 6, many of the elements of COOPERATION are designed to give users transparent access to information stored in databases and document objects. Several applications and facilities in the environment must share a set of common services to carry out these tasks. The COOPERATION Services Layer contains these common services. Figure 7-1 shows a breakout of the basic types of services available.

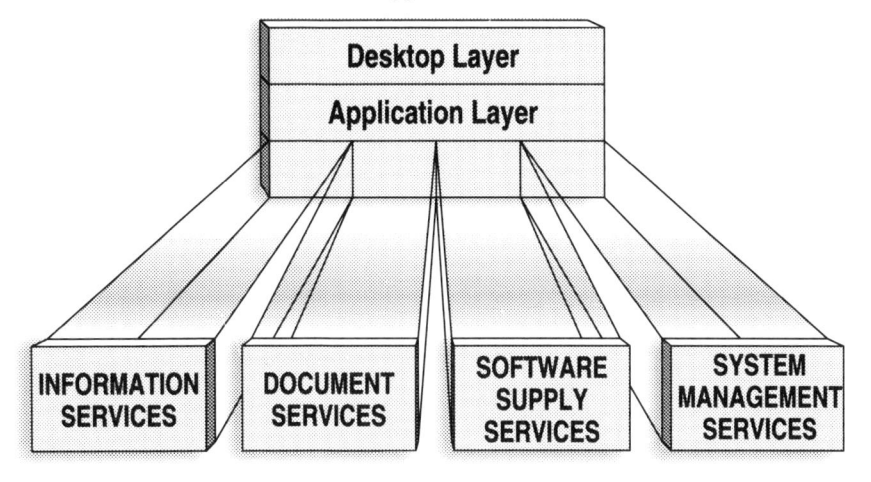

Figure 7-1: Breakout of Basic COOPERATION Services

The most significant elements of the Services Layer that are shared among applications and other COOPERATION components are those that provide transparent database access, those responsible for file storage and retrieval, those that make it possible to conduct full-text searches of information stored throughout the enterprise or work group, and those that perform document conversion. Collectively, these services are referred to as the Information Services.

Document Services are built around the organizing principle of a file cabinet with drawers and folders. Within this element of the COOPERATION Services Layer, users and system administrators can control access and efficient use of the many kinds of documents that can be stored in the COOPERATION environment.

Another important element of the COOPERATION Services Layer is the Software Supply Service. As you know, this service uses the metaphor of a supply cabinet into which applications can be stored and from which users can check them out, use them, and return them. This chapter will look in depth at how this metaphor works and how it can be used by various elements of the COOPERATION system.

The last element of the COOPERATION Services Layer we will examine in this chapter is the System Management Services component. This layer is primarily of interest to system administrators charged with the responsibility for installing and maintaining users, workstations, and the Supply Cabinet.

INFORMATION SERVICES

Many modern enterprises find themselves with multiple databases from various vendors as a result of rapid growth and the peculiar individual needs of departments and work groups. When a user needs to cross departmental boundaries to retrieve information, the process can be difficult, even impossible. COOPERATION provides database management system (DBMS) access mechanisms that make it easy for workstation users to do their jobs even when the information they need is scattered in diverse and incompatible databases.

At the heart of the COOPERATION DBMS access capabilities is a suite of three products that work together to provide easy access to databases that support the ANSI Standard Structured Query Language (SQL), notably Oracle and DB2 files:

- SQLTalk/Windows, a multi-window interactive mechanism for dynamic data access

- Express Edit, a tool that permits developers, managers, and end users to design and modify windows and screens that facilitate database access

- Report Windows, a COOPERATION component that enables all types of users to define and generate reports from the contents of one or more SQL-compatible database tables

COOPERATION includes SQLBase, a powerful OS/2 relational database on the local departmental server. SQLBase can be used in conjunction with Oracle and DB2 databases stored remotely to create efficient and effective database management applications, as shown in Figure 7-2.

System administrators make use of built-in access services to control connections between the LAN and remote SQL databases. The Oracle-compatible product performs SQL instructions and facilitates; exchanges between workstation and server, mapping messages to the specific interface of the target database. This component relies on Oracle's proprietary SQL*Net product for the network connection. SQL*Net is not part of

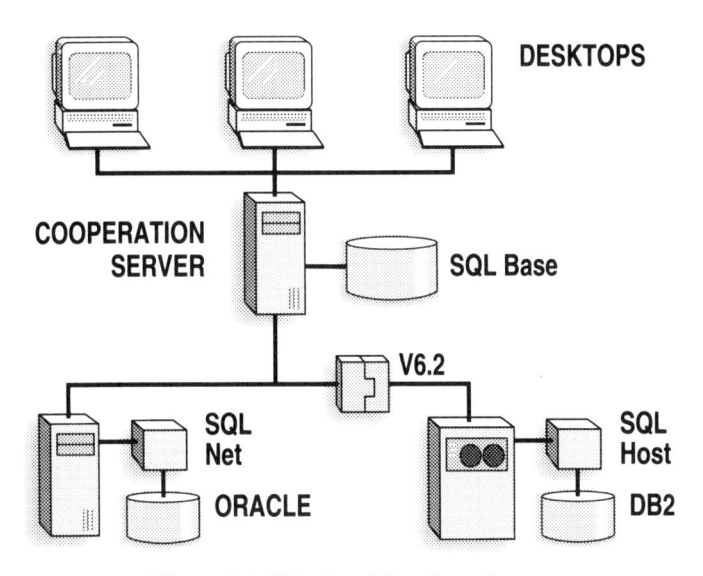

Figure: 7-2: Distributed Database Access

COOPERATION; it must be supplied by the client organization and installed on the server.

For DB2 access, system administrators have use of a gateway that connects the local server to a remote DB2 database using SNA LU6.2 protocols. On the host mainframe side of the link, Gupta's SQLHost application, not included with COOPERATION, must be installed. The link is then performed between the server and the mainframe with these two products. Like its Oracle counterpart, this COOPERATION service performs SQL instructions and exchanges between workstation and server, and from server to host, mapping messages to database contents as appropriate.

Development of applications that use these Oracle or DB2 database connections involves the use of a Standard, Advanced, or Windows Software Developer Kit level COOPERATION DBMS Access tool, as shown in Figure 7-3.

Express Edit is part of the Standard tool package, as is Report Windows. These easy-to-use components permit end users and system administrators to develop "canned" interactions with remote host systems and databases.

The Advanced tool set incorporates SQLTalk Windows and also incorporates all of the capabilities of the Standard tool group. The advanced tools facilitate the development of highly interactive terminal-interface based Oracle and DB2 applications which conduct *ad hoc* database queries that would be difficult or impossible to frame with the Standard tools.

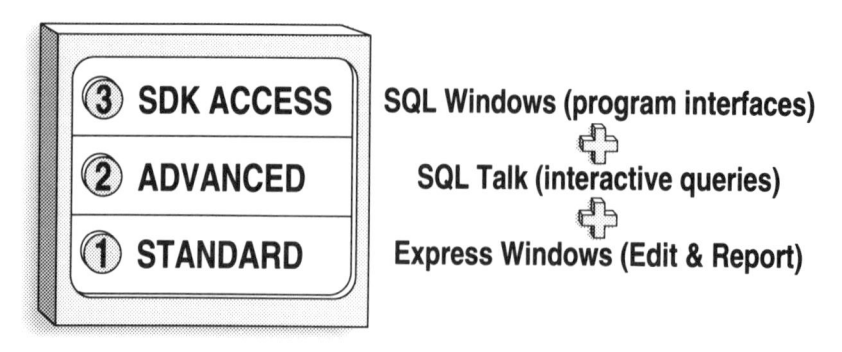

```
┌─────────────────────┐
│ ③ SDK ACCESS        │   SQL Windows (program interfaces)
├─────────────────────┤                ✚
│ ② ADVANCED          │   SQL Talk (interactive queries)
├─────────────────────┤                ✚
│ ① STANDARD          │   Express Windows (Edit & Report)
└─────────────────────┘
```

Figure 7-3: Levels of Database Application Development

For the most flexible and advanced use of the COOPERATION DBMS access services, the enterprise would choose the SDK tool. This tool encompasses all of the contents of the other two and adds a set of application programming interfaces (APIs) that allow the use of conventional programming languages such as C and C++ to create interactive database applications.

DOCUMENT RETRIEVAL SERVICES

The Information Storage Manager (ISM) in COOPERATION gives users real transparency as they store and retrieve files and/or documents from various locations throughout the enterprise. As computing systems grow and information is distributed into wider areas of the enterprise, finding specific files becomes increasingly difficult. Users must recall detailed information about these files. This problem can be avoided by the use of the ISM because it handles the tracking of file locations as well as their storage and retrieval.

ISM uses file profiles — sets of attributes about files that are automatically generated and maintained by the system — to provide efficient search and retrieval. The system administrator can define specific locations or disposition categories for documents and files and the ISM can then handle these requirements transparently to the user.

A key activity of the ISM is version control. Version profiles permit users to store multiple versions of a particular file and then retrieve the specific desired version without knowing where the document is stored.

The entire ISM component of COOPERATION is wrapped in a flexible security system that enables system administrators as well as users to control access to, use and modification of files and documents.

ORGANIZATION OF DOCUMENTS IN THE ISM

ISM uses a familiar file cabinet metaphor (see Figure 7-4) to store and manage the retrieval of documents. Independent of their physical location in the enterprise information system, documents and files are organized by:

- catalog (file cabinet)
- category (approximately equivalent to file folder)
- document

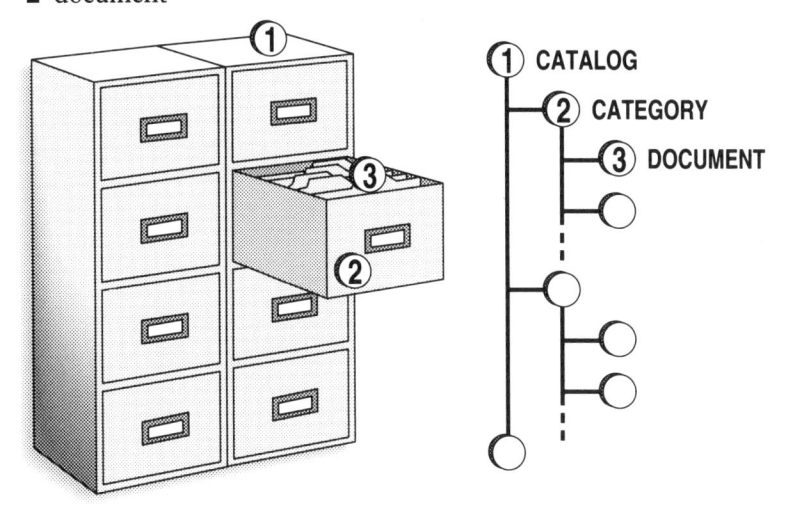

Figure 7-4: Document Management in COOPERATION

ISM stores a profile of all items it catalogs. This profile contains information about the file that facilitates its retrieval. Documents can be stored on the user's workstation or on the server or some other remote location. From the user's perspective, the differences are transparent; the user always works with the same file-retrieval dialog (see Figure 7-5) regardless of where ISM has stored the document.

Users can retrieve files based on:

- title
- creator
- last modifier
- creation date
- last modified date
- key words

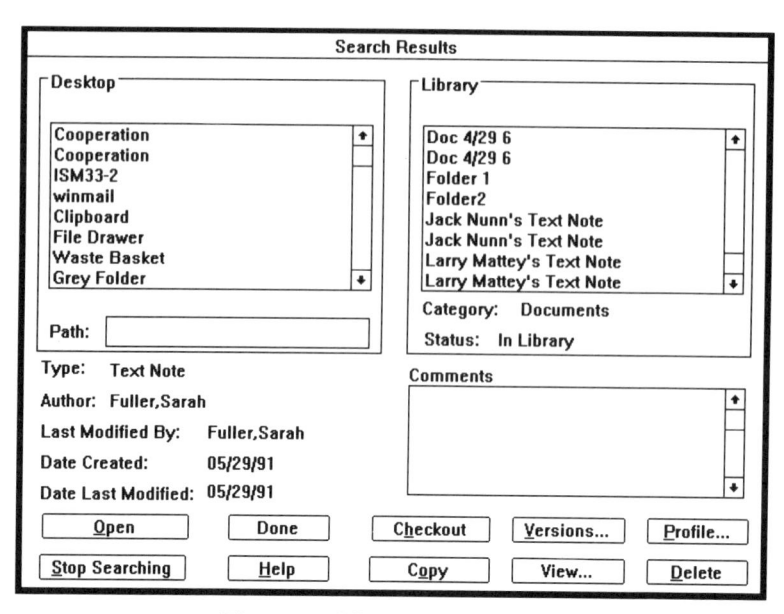

```
                        Search Results
┌─Desktop──────────────────┐  ┌─Library──────────────────┐
│ Cooperation           ▲ │  │ Doc 4/29 6            ▲ │
│ Cooperation             │  │ Doc 4/29 6              │
│ ISM33-2                 │  │ Folder 1                │
│ winmail                 │  │ Folder2                 │
│ Clipboard               │  │ Jack Nunn's Text Note   │
│ File Drawer             │  │ Jack Nunn's Text Note   │
│ Waste Basket            │  │ Larry Mattey's Text Note│
│ Grey Folder           ▼ │  │ Larry Mattey's Text Note▼│
│                         │  │ Category:  Documents    │
│ Path: [            ]    │  │ Status:    In Library   │
└─────────────────────────┘  │ Comments                │
Type:     Text Note          │                       ▲ │
Author:   Fuller,Sarah       │                         │
Last Modified By: Fuller,Sarah│                        │
Date Created:     05/29/91   │                       ▼ │
Date Last Modified: 05/29/91 └─────────────────────────┘

  [ Open ]    [ Done ]    [ Checkout ]  [ Versions... ] [ Profile... ]
  [Stop Searching] [ Help ] [ Copy ]    [ View... ]     [ Delete ]
```

Figure 7-5: File Retrieval Dialog Box

When the user presents a search to ISM, the application returns a list of all documents, regardless of storage location, to which the user has access and which meet the criteria. The user can then choose one or more of the candidate documents and check it out. Users who perform some searches frequently can create and store these queries in a document which they can use as a template for subsequent searches. The ISM maintains this library of pre-configured searches.

The ISM makes it possible for multiple users to share access to any file in the system. It tracks the work of all modifiers of the document and deals with version control transparently to the user. If the document owner enables it, the ISM will create secondary versions of a document when it needs to do so to enable it to keep versions synchronized. Typically, this means it will create a secondary version when either of the following events occurs:

- the latest primary version is open and another user wishes to access it

- the primary version is no longer the latest version accessed

As time goes on, this creation of primary and secondary files creates "version lines" (see Figure 7-6). The ISM takes care of merging changes into new versions as appropriate.

The system administrator can control the number of versions the

DOCUMENT LIBRARY

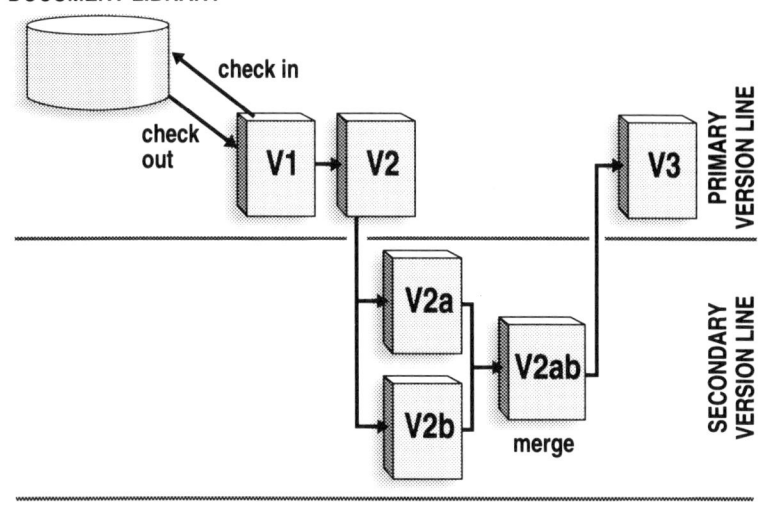

Figure 7-6: Version Flow in the ISM

system is to track for files. When a particular document's version levels exceed this limit, it is disposed of as defined by its Disposition Category Profile (discussed below). This facility permits the system administrator to prevent system performance from bogging down and disk capacity from being exhausted by obsolete documents.

The ISM relies on six profiles to provide semi-automatic and transparent management of documents.

Document profiles are used to describe files. They contain information such as the file name, author, modifiers, creation and modification dates, keywords, a list of people who are allowed various levels of access to the document, the category and disposition, an optional author-supplie synopsis of the document, and the number of versions that can be on-line at one time.

Version profiles uniquely identify each version of a file. Each version has its own profile which keeps track of the check-in/check-out status, the version, any merges that have taken place, and optional comments.

File Category Profiles are maintained by system administrators. They describe the categories of document that appear in the "Category" pop-up menu of the document profile dialog. Categories are often used to determine the storage location and disposition of documents.

A Disposition Category Profile defines what happens to file versions that become obsolete as described earlier. For example, the system administrator can define categories like trash, archive, tape backup, pending deletion, and CD-ROM. Each document is assigned a disposition category and when any version of it reaches obsolescence, disposition is as automatic as desired.

The Shelf Profile describes the physical storage locations for files. Shelves reside on the server and are controlled by the system administrator.

The Disposition Shelf Profile corresponds to the Disposition Category Profile described earlier. The system administrator defines this type of profile to define where documents which must be disposed of should be placed. Like shelves, disposition shelves reside on the server.

DOCUMENT CONVERSION

One of the most serious compatibility problems faced by many enterprises arises when users with different word processor preferences must exchange documents across the network. Each word processor has developed its own proprietary file format and there is very little compatibility among them even though they all have a significant number of features and functions in common.

COOPERATION supports document conversion at two levels. Files explicitly imported by the user to the workstation desktop are converted automatically unless the user overrides that function. This provides most users with what they want (transparent document conversion and the ability to use their chosen word processors) while allowing the option of receiving a document in the word processor format in which it was created or last modified.

Any document object handled by the system through COOPERATION Mail, Print Services, ISM, or text retrieval can be automatically and transparently converted to the user's preferred format.

When a new user is added to a COOPERATION installation, the system administrator defines, among other things, that user's default word processing format. Generally, this corresponds to the word processing application the user has chosen (or on which the work group has standardized, though such standardization is no longer a significant requirement once COOPERATION is installed).

PRINT SERVICES

COOPERATION Print Services are designed to give the user transparent access to any printer on the local LAN or elsewhere on which the user is registered. It also includes facilities for monitoring print jobs and changing some of their characteristics.

Using Print Services, users select a printer and initiate print jobs. They activate the Print Services icon, which displays a list of all printers to which the user has been granted access by the system administrator. The default printer for the user's work group or area is highlighted. Once a printer has been chosen, the user simply drags the object to be printed to the Print Services tool on the desktop to initiate the print job.

When the print job is in process, the user can use the Network Print View tool to:

- determine the status of their print jobs
- pause, resume, or delete print jobs they own
- change priorities of their print jobs
- rearrange the order of printing jobs they own
- look at print queue statistics
- receive help about the Print Services

The Network Print Viewer tool (see Figure 7-7) is also responsible for notifying the user workstation if a job owned by its user is halted because of printer problems.

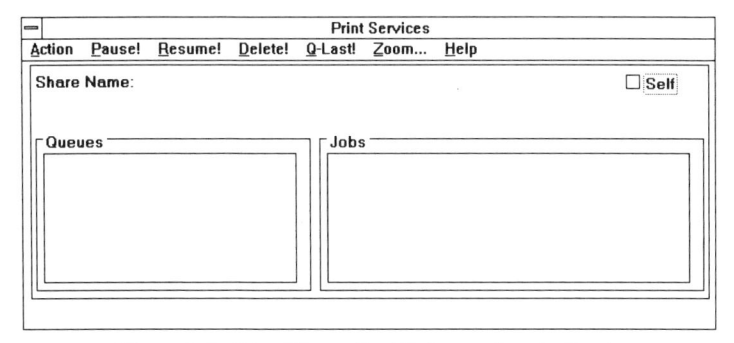

Figure 7-7: Print Viewer Tool Software Supply Service

SOFTWARE SUPPLY SERVICE

Many organizations face a dilemma when it comes time to purchase application packages. Programs that are used constantly by some or all users on the network or in the enterprise pose no problem; one copy must be obtained for each user, whether by individual or bulk purchase or through a site licensing relationship.

But what about programs that are used by many different users, but to which few or no users require constant or continual access? It is clearly inefficient for the organization to purchase enough copies so that each user can have access to the application for the infrequent occasions when it is needed. But software licensing provisions generally prohibit the installation of a single copy of an application on more than one computer at a time.

For example, a company might wish to make available a program that assists managers in the completion of semi-annual employee performance evaluation forms. The company might have dozens of managers who will wish to use the application, but each of these users will only need access to the application for a few hours every six months.

With the COOPERATION Software Supply Cabinet, the enterprise can buy enough copies of this application so that any manager who wishes to use a copy can check it out, use it, and return it when his or her task is complete. By purchasing the right number of copies, the enterprise can avoid any manager not being able to access the program when needed, while avoiding the excessive expense of having a one-copy-per-manager situation.

The Supply Cabinet Service permits the system administrator to install software on the server, determine which users or groups can have access to the applications, and keep track of the number of copies on hand, checked out, and available.

Users who wish to check out an application go to the Supply Cabinet on the server, select the application they want (if it is available) and simply install the program on their workstations. The installed application appears on their desktop in a form that depends on its degree of integration into COOPERATION. When they finish using the program, they simply de-install it.

The system administrator can determine at any time who has checked out each copy of the application and when it was checked out so that if a user has finished using the program but simply forgotten to return it to the Supply Cabinet, the system administrator can send the user a polite reminder to de-install the program so others can use it. (In fact, the system administrator could create an agent task, as discussed in Chapter 3, to handle this task practically automatically and transparently.)

Release 1.0 of COOPERATION is well-suited to this type of management for DOS applications that are bridged or integrated into the environment. Applications that run under Windows are harder to manage with the Supply Cabinet because of the greater complexity of installing and de–installing Windows Applications.

SYSTEM MANAGEMENT SERVICES

The System Management Services aspect of the COOPERATION Services Layer is primarily of interest to system administrators. It consists of two primary and several minor sets of functions. Of the primary functions on which we will spend some time, one deals with configuration and installation issues and one handles security.

These two types of services have some things in common. Both are placed under the control of a system administrator who typically is assigned responsibility for a LAN installation (single or multi-server). And both use dialog boxes on the system administrator's COOPERATION desktop to set parameters and control functions.

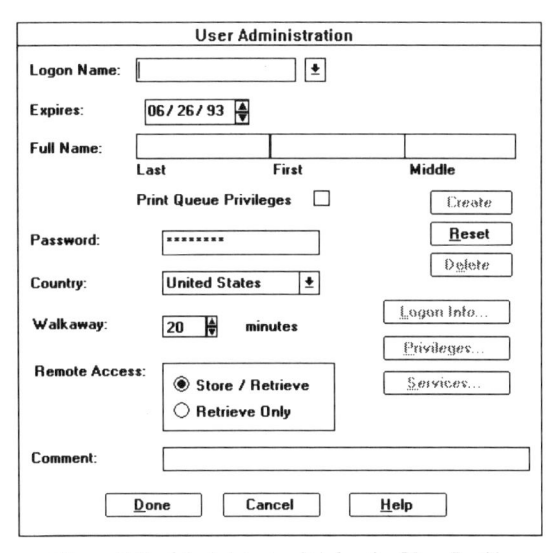

Figure 7-8: Administrator Dialog for User Profile

CONFIGURATION AND INSTALLATION

The key to installation of new workstations and users on the COOPERATION network is the User Profile, which is controlled from a dialog box like the one shown in Figure 7-8.

Each user has primary access to at least one workstation on the system and may have such access to multiple workstations. On any workstation where the user has such access, the system administrator must place a user profile. There is also a version of the profile on the server, which is considered the "correct" one in the event of a conflict between two or more other versions.

As you can see from Figure 7-8, the User Profile contains information about the user that includes:

- User ID (user's sign-on identification for the system)
- Full Name
- Password
- Screen Time-out (used by workstation's "Walkaway" tool)
- Account Expires (date on which a temporary user of the system is no longer able to access the workstation)
- Password Last Changed (date when user last changed passwords)

- Last Logon (date and time user last logged on)
- Next Change Available (soonest date user may change passwords)
- Failed Logon Count (number of unsuccessful logon attempts by the user)
- Password Expires (date user's password expires)

Each user is also associated with a Logon Restrictions profile. The system administrator establishes and maintains these profiles, which are stored on the server. They enable the administrator to define the workstations to which a user has access and the dates and times the user may be active on the system. Through another profile, the system administrator may also lock a user out of specific workstations.

A COOPERATION system administrator is also responsible for managing groups of users who are treated for some purposes as a single unit. The system administrator handles this task through the dialog shown in Figure 7-9.

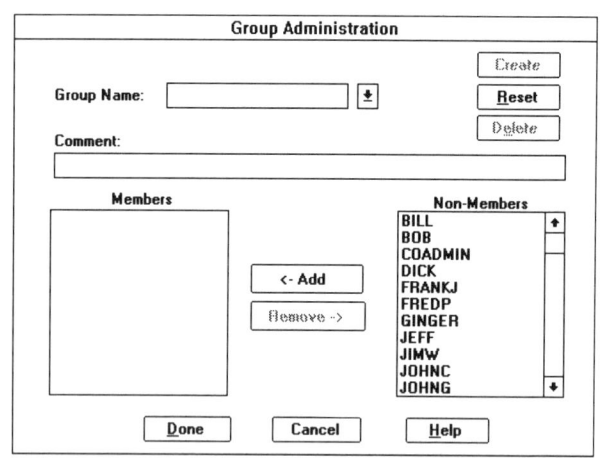

Figure 7-9: Group Profile Configuration Dialog

Group profiles contain information about the group and a list of all members and specific non-members. By moving a user's name from one list to the other, the system administrator can quickly and easy reconfigure a group.

Through similar dialogs, system administrators configure and control:

- individual workstations
- workstation access permissions
- servers
- printers and their associated print queues

SECURITY MANAGEMENT

Security is a major concern for most organizations and a point of flexibility in COOPERATION. Most networked systems are characterized by one of two situations:

- excellent data security with very little user control, involvement, or flexibility

- highly flexible control by users with a resulting lack of real security at the system level

COOPERATION achieves a blend of both solid security at the server and system level with the ability for users to control — within broad parameters — access to objects they control. It accomplishes this because of the object-oriented nature of the environment, which permits a very fine level of granularity with respect to security. Access control is simply an attribute of all COOPERATION objects. An object's owner can control who has access to the object and at what level. All objects that are not owned by a particular user are controlled by the system administrator.

System administrators can control security at two levels.

First, as we saw briefly in the previous section, they can establish workstation access parameters for users, set expiration dates on passwords, and manage a number of other system-wide controls that involve security.

Second, they can control a number of aspects of password design and usage, including such things as:

- minimum password length

- minimum and maximum password age

System administrators can use their control over password parameters to deal with what may be attempts to breach security in the system as well. They may, for example, define the following parameters:

- the length of time that can transpire before a user will be forced off the system if he or she is in violation of logon restrictions

- the number of times a user can attempt to log on unsuccessfully before the workstation becomes inaccessible for a specified period

COOPERATION assists the user with workstation security without any necessity for the user to do anything. With the "Walkaway" tool, COOPERATION causes the workstation to go into a temporarily inaccessible state when it detects no user activity (keystrokes or mouse movement) for a specified period of time. The user must then enter a password to regain control of the workstation. This prevents other people from accessing a workstation during the user's absence.

OTHER SYSTEM MANAGEMENT SERVICES

COOPERATION has facilities for system administrators to manage and assist users with other system-related activities. These include:

- archive and restore capabilities that permit users to perform full desktop and office backups and, thereafter, incremental backups of files, with a reasonable degree of transparency
- diagnostic tools on the system administrator's desktop to deal with exceptions, errors, and other conditions requiring the administrator's attention and possible intervention.

8
Strategies for Deployment

This chapter focuses on the design issues involved in implementing a COOPERATION installation. It begins with a discussion of how to organize at all levels of the enterprise for the acceptance and integration of COOPERATION. As you can appreciate by now, this process has implications throughout the organization. Careful planning will greatly smooth the conversion.

We then present a seven-step process, or methodology, for the design and deployment of COOPERATION in any given department of the enterprise. In the Epilogue we will explore ways to scale up this deployment strategy to the entire enterprise.

The chapter concludes with a discussion of how you can use COOPERATION to solve real business problems by following the methodological model presented and summarizes the advantages of this approach.

ORGANIZING FOR COOPERATION

This section discusses the keys to success with COOPERATION and suggests some aspects of top-management buy-in that should be established at the outset of this project. The critical success factors are summarized in Figure 8-1.

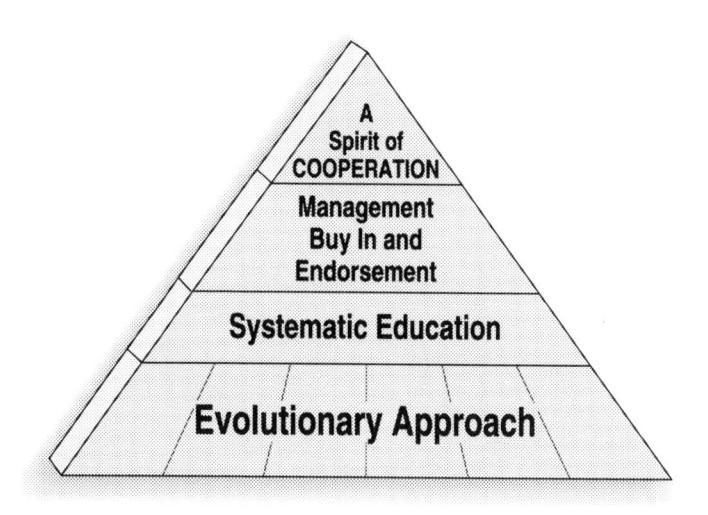

Figure 8-1: Critical Success Factors for Deployment

THE SPIRIT OF COOPERATION

The key to success is not simply to "computerize" existing activities, using machines to perform routine tasks faster. Rather it is to analyze how your business works, capture that knowledge in a working model of the enterprise, then build management solutions on top of that model to enhance both the efficiency *and* the effectiveness of your operations.

Achieving qualitative gains of this sort requires improving the way individuals interact to get cooperative work done in your company. COOPERATION was specifically designed to facilitate these cooperative efforts.

MANAGEMENT BUY-IN

No enterprise-wide undertaking can succeed without the solid support of top management. These managers must understand the attainable goals of adoptive COOPERATION and they must clearly and visibly support the process at every step. In the absence of such support, employees will find themselves being diverted from tasks related to the installation of the new COOPERATION system onto other tasks perceived by management as having greater priority. Consequently, employees will have the impression that this project is not very important, and they will be less inclined to spend their limited time and energy on ensuring its success.

Adopting COOPERATION involves the expenditure of dollars as well as the allocation of people. Here again, top management must clearly and publicly signal its support of the process by funding the project adequately so that the message to employees involved in the process is quite clear.

At the beginning of the project, it would be a good idea to have the senior manager in the group where COOPERATION is being installed send a detailed memo of support to every individual in the organization who might be affected by the project. Even better, get this manager to speak to the assembled personnel and communicate his or her enthusiastic support.

EARLY USER EDUCATION

Once top management has given the go-ahead, you should immediately begin educating users about the goals and implications of adopting COOPERATION. People are often frightened of and, therefore, resistant to new technologies and systems. It is important that these fears be openly discussed and resolved early in the adoption process.

One thing to emphasize to users whose working lives are about to be changed is the fact that COOPERATION, unlike other automation experiences they may have had, is specifically designed to facilitate cooperation between people. It is not a process of turning people into automatons, but rather a technology to facilitate the way they already work and to make them more productive and effective employees.

AN EVOLUTIONARY APPROACH

The ultimate goal of COOPERATION is to transform your organization by facilitating virtually all of your interactions, allowing your entire company to operate directly on line with a clarity and swiftness that will quickly leave your competition behind.

However, this is not a goal that can be achieved overnight. Transforming your company into a fully cooperative environment will require the investment of considerable time and effort. Ideally, you should realize a return on your investment very quickly, making the adoption of COOPERATION as profitable as possible.

You will undoubtedly make mistakes as you go, and you should have an opportunity to learn from those mistakes as early as possible so you can minimize their impact. It hardly makes sense to spend two years building a model of your operations, only to discover that the model is unworkable when you finally begin to use it!

For these reasons, we do not recommend that you analyze your entire business and attempt to move it onto the COOPERATION platform in a single effort. Rather, we advocate a phased adoption strategy, as described in Chapter 5. Start with a select set of departments and apply COOPERATION to their operations. As you roll COOPERATION out into other departments, apply what you learned with the initial departments to achieve optimum results.

In this chapter, we present a seven-step process for applying COOPERATION to a single department. At the end of the chapter, we offer some suggestions for scaling up COOPERATION to apply to the business as a whole.

Please bear in mind as you read these steps that there is nothing sacred about them. You can change the sequence in some cases, move forward and backward in the process to improve on decisions made in earlier steps, or insert additional steps that make sense in your own business. Moreover, the process is never as linear as this description would suggest. Rather, there is considerable iteration through the stages as the results of each stage clarify what should have been done in earlier stages.

In short, what follows is not so much a fixed recipe as a set of flexible guidelines for achieving success through COOPERATION. The basic sequence of steps, as introduced in Chapter 1, is summarized in Figure 8-2.

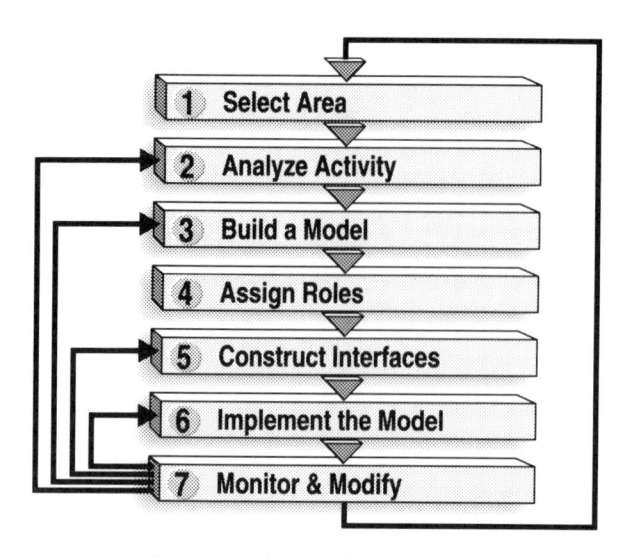

Figure 8-2: A Seven–Step Methodology

1. Select Area
2. Analyze Activity
3. Build a Model
4. Assign Roles
5. Construct Interfaces
6. Implement the Model
7. Monitor & Modify

STEP ONE: CHOOSING A DEPARTMENT

Choosing the right department for your initial deployment is essential to getting off to a good start. Here are some considerations you should bear in mind as you decide where to deploy COOPERATION technology first:

1. ROUTINE OPERATIONS

Tackle a department with lots of well-understood routine forms, procedures, and other elements that you can readily capture and automate. For example, the purchasing department might be a good place to start because it has many well-defined procedures. By contrast, a research department might not be as good a choice because so much of its functioning depends on informal, unstructured interactions among research personnel.

2. WELL-DEFINED ROLES

It's also a good idea to start with a department that has clearly defined roles. For example, the payroll group probably has payroll clerks who enter data into the system, other clerks who are clearly responsible for interviewing employees and managers, and a clearly defined hierarchy of control. By contrast, the functions of the marketing communications group involve its staff in a wide range of roles that are not always predictable. A person might play a public relations role one day and act as a document production manager the next. This department is generally not as well suited to a first-pass implementation of the system but is an excellent candidate later.

COOPERATION uses information about roles to simplify the processes of communication and workflow automation, so selecting a department with well-defined roles will allow COOPERATION to bring you the greatest benefits as quickly as possible.

3. HIGH VISIBILITY

The department you begin with should be one with sufficient enterprise-wide visibility and impact that a success in its enhancement with COOPERATION will create an example other departments will wish to follow. Make sure the chosen department is central to business operations. Once COOPERATION is in place, this department's interactions with other departments will make it clear to everyone how much better this department is functioning. On the other hand, don't select a department that requires massive integration with other departments, as that will slow up process both technologically and politically.

4. POTENTIAL BENEFIT

Choose a department where automating workflow and supporting team activities will have a major impact on both the efficiency and effectiveness of that group.

There is often confusion about the differences between efficiency and effectiveness. These differences are summed up in the witticism that, "Efficiency is doing things right; effectiveness is doing the right thing." An organization can be terribly efficient at turning out a product nobody wants to buy or providing a service for which the market has long since disappeared. Its efficiency is beyond question, but the results are not very helpful to the company's stockholders or employees. On the other hand, a company that has the right product or service or approach to the market and operates inefficiently loses profit margin and eventually market share to a competitor who sees the same need but is able to fill it more profitably by being more efficient.

The department you pick should be one that has a product or service to deliver and where improvements in the selection, design, or refinement of that product or service can have a clear impact on the profitability of the enterprise. Note that this product or service can and often will be one that is delivered to an in-house clientele rather than to external customers.

5. TYPICAL ACTIVITIES

If possible, it's a good idea to select a department that is fairly representative of the organization, in the sense that it deals with objects and processes that are common to many other departments. This will cause you to think through many generic issues that will come up as you move from the initial department into other areas of the company. It will also maximize the reuse of the business objects you create in your first model, speeding the later deployment of the technology.

For example, you would probably find that almost any department with an administrative role would be a good candidate for an early COOPERATION department. This department deals with forms, documents, a defined work flow, and other objects that have significant characteristics in common with the rest of the enterprise. On the other hand, few if any departments outside R&D have to deal with lab books, patents, and other kinds of documents and objects peculiar to its research role.

6. ABILITY TO WITHSTAND DISRUPTION

No matter how good the technology, computerizing a department usually creates some delays and disruptions. If you try your first deployment of COOPERATION in a department that simply has to run smoothly at all times, you are bound to create more problems than you need to.

For example, it would be unwise for a manufacturing company to start using COOPERATION for shop floor management because this is not an area that can tolerate delays without costing the company significant revenues. The personnel department, while no less essential, might be better able to withstand the temporary disruptions of the conversion process. Once the process of implementing COOPERATION is better understood in the enterprise, of course, the shop floor might be a great place for a subsequent deployment of COOPERATION and provide even greater returns.

STEP TWO: ANALYZING THE BUSINESS ACTIVITY

The second step is to perform a detailed analysis of how the selected department operates on a day-to-day basis. The department's workflow may not be completely explicit; much of it typically is found in the heads of people rather than in procedure manuals. Moreover, these people may not be consciously aware of what they know about workflow and how they use it. Your job is to tease this information out of their minds, sometimes even their subconscious. Even if the real workflow is inefficient or difficult to fathom, it is the place you must start in deploying COOPERATION in the department.

It is important in this step that you quantify as much of the department's processing as possible. Knowing how long it takes for some steps to be performed, how many steps are inserted between the beginning and end of a goal, how many hand-offs take place before processing is complete and other such information will help you in your post-installation assessment of the value of the project.

AVOIDING CLASSIC BIASES

To suggest such an analysis immediately begs the question of what kind of analytical tools should be applied. Resist the temptation to use the information tools you already know. They are bound to lead you astray in at least two ways.

First, conventional analysis tools are oriented toward either data or procedures. For example, information engineering is strongly data-centered, documenting the structure and flow of information as it proceeds through a department. By contrast, functional decomposition is biased toward procedures, breaking high-level operations into increasingly detailed operations until the operations are sufficiently obvious to reduce them to program code. (Figure 8-3)

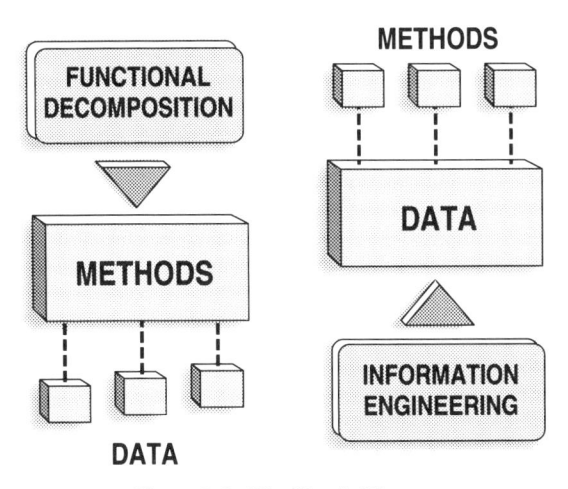

Figure 8-3: The Classic Biases

These biases are hardly surprising given that procedures and data have been supported by entirely different technologies in the past—namely, programs and databases, respectively. With object technology, this arbitrary boundary is erased. Procedures and data that go together are bound together into the same object, and objects become the new unit of analysis. This new unit demands new analytical tools. We will have a specific recommendation on this point shortly.

The second problem with conventional techniques is that they violate the encapsulation of objects. It is the responsibility of a document object to accept, contain, and print out the contents of a document. It is of no concern to any other object in the system how the document object carries out these responsibilities. In particular, other objects should have no idea when a document is using variables as opposed to relying on methods. To make this kind of information accessible or, worse yet, important to other objects would make the system much more complicated and harder to manage.

BECOME AN OBSERVER

The best technique is to approach the problem like a scientist—try to observe with as little bias and as few pre-existing analytical categories as possible. Simply observe and record what people do as they conduct their everyday activities. Track the flow of paperwork and communication. Be sure to check for activities which might not occur within the time window of the observations, such as budgeting or annual reviews.

This observational phase also consists of monitoring work habits, reading policies and procedures manuals, and scanning memos and other directives that affect departmental procedures. In general, the members of the analysis team should do as much homework as they can before beginning interviews with department staff so they can conserve the time and energies of the people in the department. This, in turn, will enable them to glean as much accurate information from the interviews as possible.

Incidentally, it is important that the people who do the analysis and subsequent interviewing should be the same individuals who will actually construct the model of the department's operation. This avoids further transfers of information, which can introduce confusion and misunderstanding.

WORKING WITH CONTENT EXPERTS

Doing this homework will allow the analysis team to ask more informed, intelligent questions and thereby establish greater respect and rapport with their clientele. This is crucial because building and installing a working model of the department is not a trivial process. The ultimate users of the system must be interrupted as little as possible during this process to avoid disrupting the function of the department.

When the observation phase is complete, move to the interview phase.

Select a subset of people in the targeted department to serve as experts on the content of the procedures and systems. Work with the manager or supervisory personnel to select the most informed individuals. This will reinforce the importance of the modeling effort and maximizing support for it.

Establish rapport with the content experts early in the analysis phase. Open honesty is not only acceptable, it is essential. For example, these people need to know that you expect them to talk about where policies are not actually followed. Your interest is in creating a model of how the organization actually works, not of how it is supposed to work. The two are often out of synchronization at many points. Capture the actual model first. Then you can think about improving it.

Ask people how things work, what are the critical steps, how do things really get done, how these processes differ from official policy, what are the current bottlenecks, and what suggestions would they have for improvement. You may also want to interview people in some of the departments that work with the targeted department to understand what they expect from it and how they perceive its operations.

As team members conduct these interviews, they must bear in mind that most experts have difficulty articulating their expertise. This is largely because it is automatic and unconscious. In fact, many people believe that a true expert is someone who has sublimated much of his or her knowledge so that it is not something that is usually in the expert's consciousness. That's one reason you study behavior before conducting interviews—people may not even realize what they are doing! You may have to ask the same question several times and in different ways until a meaningful and consistent answer emerges.

DEALING WITH OFFICIAL POLICIES

There will probably be many discrepancies between official policies and the way things are actually done. How these discrepancies are dealt with is up to each company, but here are some considerations:

- If you build a model only to match the official policies and ignore actual practice, you won't have a true working model. As a result, the model won't actually support what people are doing, and it will likely fail.

- If you build only to match actual practice, the model will support the department much more effectively. However, it will also tend to condone deviations from policy, which is bound to offend upper management.

The best approach is probably to work with upper management to bring the two different sets of practices into alignment before completing the analysis, as shown in Figure 8-4. Often, people deviate from perfectly valid policies simply to avoid paperwork and other tedious detail. If that workflow is automated, then getting people to adhere to the policy should not be a serious problem because you will have taken the hassle out of conforming to the policy.

On the other hand, many policies reflect outmoded management procedures that should have been retired long ago. In these cases, you should be on the alert for "deviant procedures" that may actually reflect better solutions to management problems. If they do, you want not only to capture them in the workflow for the current department but also to generalize them to the company as a whole and make the new procedure official policy.

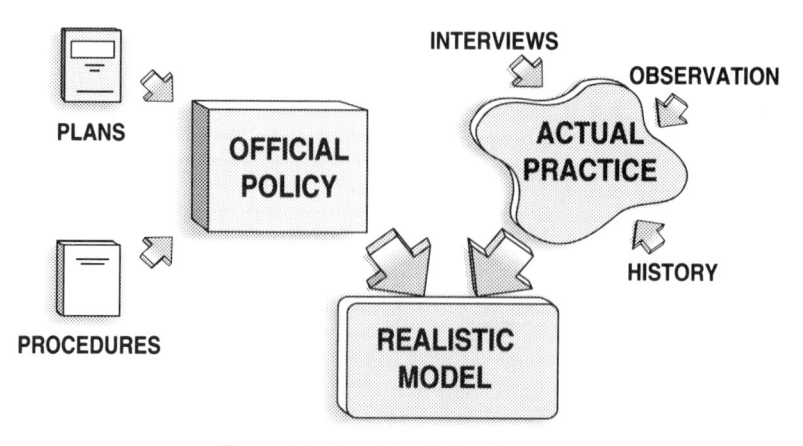

Figure 8-4: Resolving Policy Deviations

ASSEMBLING THE RESULTS

When you are finished, you should be able to answer the basic journalism questions: who, what, when, where, why, and how. Specifically, you should document:

1. What are the basic tasks carried out by the department?
2. When are they carried out? What triggers them—the passage of time, or specific events? If it's time, what is the frequency? If it's events, what kinds of events can trigger the process?
3. Who carries out these tasks? What are the hand-offs?
4. What are the dependencies among the various steps? What happens if one of them isn't completed on time?

Notice that there are no applications being specified here. What we are analyzing is the way the business works—not the specific "programs" that will be required to carry out these operations. Deciding which aspects to computerize and how to do that is a late decision in this methodology, not an early one. The main thing we need to do is anticipate the full range of activities carried out within the department so that we don't get stuck with any surprises when we use the model to support the department.

STEP THREE: DESIGNING THE MODEL

Once you have a fairly thorough analysis in hand, it's time to start turning that analysis into a model of the department. There are many published techniques for carrying out object-oriented design, and you are free to choose among them as you see fit. However, our experience has shown that one method, known as *responsibility-driven design*, has important advantages over other techniques when used to build COOPERATION models.

RESPONSIBILITY-DRIVEN DESIGN

That the key to responsibility-driven design is to think in terms of the responsibilities objects are assigned within a system. One object may be responsible for knowing how many Mark VI widgets were sold in 1992; another may be responsible for ensuring that capital expenditures receive the proper sequence of approvals. Both objects should be free to use methods and data in any way they choose to fulfill these responsibilities.

Note that this approach is substantially different from conventional software design, which tends to place most responsibility into a "main" function and to use subroutines as dumb servants. As noted earlier, it is also quite different from the traditional data-driven analytical methods in that it focuses on real-world objects, combining process and data rather than making data relationships central to the analysis (see Figure 8-5).

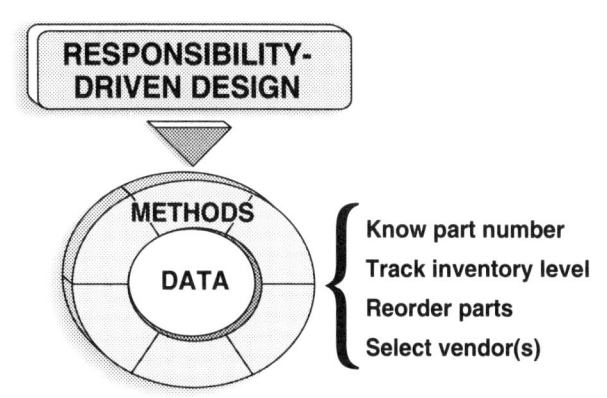

Figure 8-5: Responsibility–Driven Design

For example, a part object may be responsible for obtaining information about its inventory level. The model must be designed in such a way that no other object knows or cares how the part object gets that data. COOPERATION facilitates this kind of encapsulation of objects and behavior. For example, thanks to the design of the Information Storage Manager, no user needs to worry about where a file is stored (or even that there is such a thing as a file). Users simply open existing objects and COOPERATION takes care of the rest of the process.

An important step in this approach is to do role-playing walk-throughs of the model, with each person playing the part of an object carrying out its responsibilities. Ideally, the content experts who actually do these things everyday would play out the roles they do in their actual jobs. This helps ensure that each object object really captures the appropriate responsibilities.

Incidentally, there is a bias in our society, promulgated by the scientific community, against anthropomorphism, in which inanimate objects are treated as though they have human qualities. In fact, this is the best possible approach to take in these walk-throughs because objects do act rather like people, responding to their environments and carrying out tasks in as independent, responsible manner as they can. Moreover, getting people to personally identify with the objects they handle in the walk-through forces a level of detailed thinking that might not otherwise take place.

For a full treatment of the methodology we prefer for designing the model, we recommend the book *Designing Object-Oriented Software* by Wirfs-Brock, Wilkerson & Wiener (Prentice Hall, 1990)

INVENT ACTIVE OBJECTS

As you design the model, try to create objects that play an active role and to describe them as if they actually behave as if they were "alive," even when to do so stretches what seems to you to be the "reality" a little.

For example, in traditional data-driven design, a personnel requisition is moved or transferred from place to place. In your design, think and talk of this object as moving itself from place to place rather than waking up an application whose responsibility it is to move the requisition.

This new way of thinking about software takes some practice and may feel unnatural at first, but it greatly improved the quality of the resulting design.

STEP FOUR: ASSIGNING ROLES

Within an organization, individuals play many different roles. Some individuals have one clearly defined role while others may wear many hats. Articulating specific roles at this stage of the project will help to clarify exactly what is needed for people to be able to work with the COOPERATION when it is in place.

It is important that roles be differentiated from people. Each role may well be assigned to more than one person. For example, there may be 23 people in the department who all have the role of Benefits Clerk. For the most part, these peoples' COOPERATION roles and environments will look largely the same.

It is also important that roles not be confused with job titles. Sometimes a role is more specific than a job title. For example, one Benefits Clerk might actually be the only person in the department who processes a particular type of form (such as personnel evaluation forms). On the other hand, it is probably also true that at least some of the people with the title

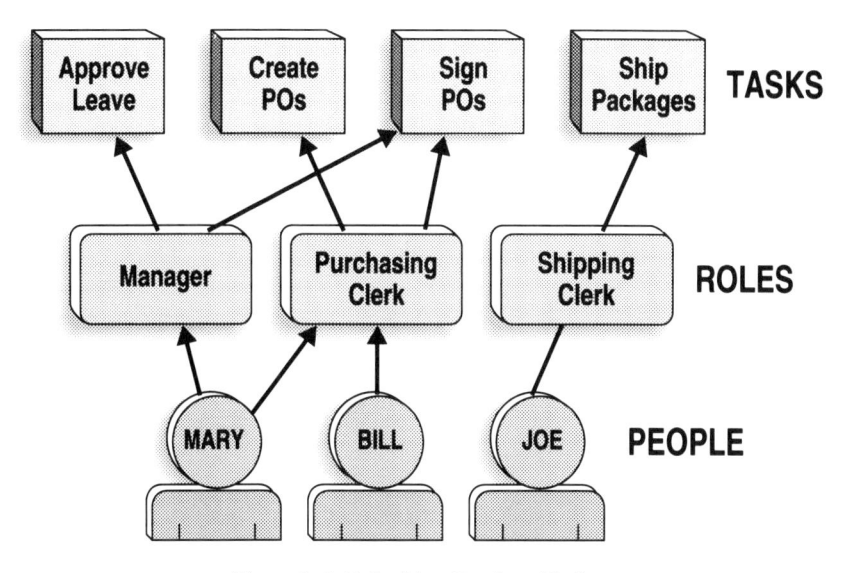

Figure 8-6: Roles Map People to Tasks

"Benefits Clerk" have other roles they play in the organization, such as team leader or member of a task force.

COOPERATION supports these different approaches to role assignment and management in a number of ways. We have examined many of them in this book. For example, as we saw in Chapter 7, the system administrator can assign people to various groups, which can in turn be granted access to certain kinds of applications and documents as a group.

EACH STEP IS A ROLE

You should begin by creating, naming, and describing a role for each step in a corporate activity. The most significant part of the description is a definition of what kinds of objects are needed for the role to be carried out.

Having defined these various roles, you will be able to create a COOPERATION desktop design for each role that contains only the things a user with that role will require. Since, as we have seen, COOPERATION supports multiple desktops, users can play multiple roles in the organization quite effectively by assigning one role per desktop.

Note, too, that the packaging of the role with a desktop will permit you to ensure that users have access to only that portion of the corporate policies and procedures library — that voluminous 16-foot shelf that everyone dreads having to consult — as they need for their job. The potential time savings here is immense.

MINIMIZE THE NUMBER OF ROLES

Having defined roles for all of the steps in the corporate process being modeled, you should step back and look for commonalties among roles that will enable you to simplify the design. Many distinct roles may still be required, but the fewer you have to design, the easier it will be for people to learn them (and, not coincidentally, the easier it will be for the implementation team to build and deploy them as well as train people on their use).

As a rule of thumb, people in the department who perform only a single role all day, such as a benefits clerk, will obviously have a dedicated role in the system. By contrast, a manger, who probably plays numerous roles in the course of a day or week, could end up with a proliferation of desktops if you don't keep efficiency in mind as you build the design.

STEP FIVE: CONSTRUCTING INTERFACES

The point of building working business models is to facilitate the construction of flexible, dynamic solutions. By capturing the basic logic of the organization in a common layer, business solutions consist largely of interfaces that operate on the model to observe or control its behavior. As a result, adding a new business solution to a COOPERATION environment may require nothing more than constructing the appropriate interfaces.

Interfaces come in two flavors: user interfaces and procedural interfaces. The former deal with the way things appear on the display and permit the user to interact with objects. The latter deal with the ways in which processes connect between objects, between tasks, and even between desktops. We will discuss each of these types of interface in turn.

DESKTOP INTERFACE CONSIDERATIONS

Each COOPERATION tool has an interface. Many tools, such as the database access system and the Business Information Monitor, include the ability to create or customize user interfaces to deal with the data and issues with which they operate.

The user is in charge of the appearance of the desktop. But you can start users out in the right direction if you focus on creating an environment that is familiar, comfortable, and clean. The variety of desktops you may need to build precludes the possibility of providing any rules for this interface design process, but we can offer some hints.

1. Group Related Objects

Users generally work with document objects in a related series of steps. Once such objects are created, users typically want to proofread them and then print them and perhaps mail them to other users. So group the Dictionary, Print Services, and In and Out Tray objects on the desktop together. Otherwise, the user will waste time and mouse motion looking for the right place to drop an object to be printed or mailed.

Similarly, if you create multiple folders, keep related topics together. Don't have a folder containing personnel forms in one place on the desktop and another folder containing related procedure files on another part of the desktop.

2. Minimize the Number of Folders

Put folders inside other folders wherever such an organization makes sense. The user won't appreciate having to sift through a lot of clutter on the desktop.

If, for example, you have a folder for pending personnel requisitions, another for requisitions that are on hold awaiting budgetary approval and another for requisitions that are not yet ready to be filed, put them all into a common Personnel Requisitions folder. You should also put the Personnel Requisition Master object in the same folder.

3. Keep Things the Same Between Desktops

If the user's roles dictate the design and implementation of multiple desktops, be sure that objects that are shared across the desktops like the wastebasket tool and calendars, appear in the same place on all desktops. Users become quickly acclimated to the location of things on their desktops; you can take advantage of this fact by keeping things between desktops as similar as the different configurations and requirements allow.

Users and system administrators who write scripts in the COOPERATION Agent Task Language can create dialog boxes through which agents can interrogate users to find out what they want done and how they want the task carried out. These dialogs should follow the basic "look and feel" of other COOPERATION dialogs: minimize the number and variety of objects in a dialog and be sure that each dialog has only a single task to accomplish. These tasks can, of course, be arbitrarily complex and involve a variety of settings. But they should not mix tasks that are either unrelated or seen by the user as separate steps or parts of a process or action.

PROCEDURAL INTERFACES

Since the department you are modeling has multiple roles and since these roles are in some sense related, you must give some thought to the hand-offs and other aspects of the procedural interface as objects flow through the system.

For example, in a personnel requisition scenario, you might have a requestor (the person who creates a personnel request and is probably outside the department), an intake clerk who enters the requisition into the system, a recruiter who looks at requirements and tries to match them up with applicants, a manager who signs requisitions and creates new job entries for the corporate human resources database, and perhaps other individuals. In designing the graphic user interface for this system, you will, of course, have captured all of the forms and other objects as icons, placed them into appropriate folder structures, and perhaps automated some of their desktop processing via agent scripts.

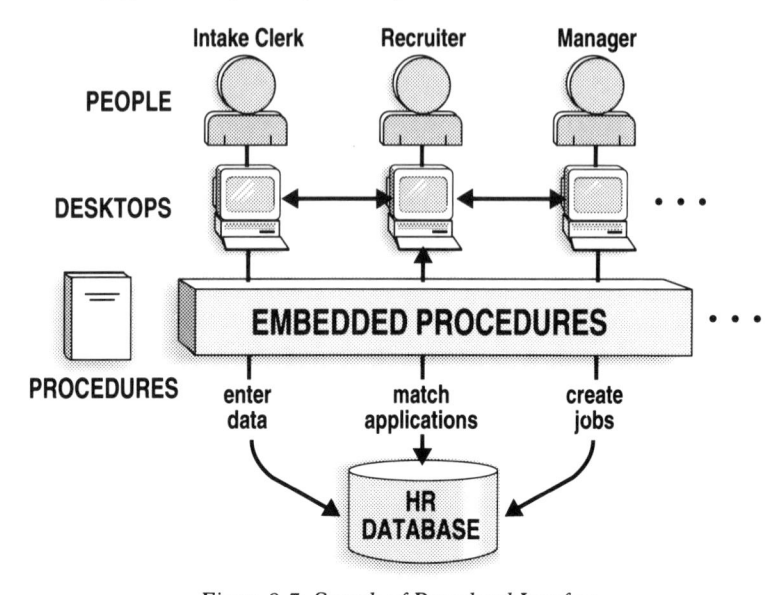

Figure 8-7: Sample of Procedural Interface

When the entry clerk finishes entering the requisition—a step that will become unnecessary as soon as the requestor's department is hooked into COOPERATION—the requisition object should be brought to the attention of the appropriate recruiting staff. You could easily design an Agent Task Language script that would accomplish this task and permit the clerk to trigger the action either with a menu choice or by pressing a button in a dialog that pops up from a script to remind the clerk of the necessity of passing on the requisition.

Many of the procedural interfaces in an organization combine control and reporting functions. The clerk enters the data into a document and creates a requisition (perhaps by clicking on the requisition object and selecting a menu choice). The recruiter might have a script or other interface through which a list of current openings meeting certain criteria could be brought into a document being created for a report.

In a multi-department situation these interfaces might well involve multiple models. For example, a concurrent engineering requirement which raises the level of cooperation between manufacturing and engineering will need to access both groups' models to be successful.

STEP SIX: EXECUTING THE DESIGN

The next step in the process of implementing COOPERATION is to build the model. This is where traditional software issues begin to arise for the first time. Notice how late in the process we have been able to postpone such issues and decisions.

THE MODEL-BUILDING PROCESS

Building the model to execute the design requires the following steps:

- build the classes using dedicated class constructors (individuals assigned the task of translating roles and objects into class structures)
- assemble the classes into a model
- plug the model into the interfaces (user and procedural)
- iteratively test and modify the model

USING DEDICATED CLASS CONSTRUCTORS

Most models are constructed by the people who design them. This tactic works well with small projects, which may involve no more than eight or ten programmers. With large projects, however, some means must be found to divide the effort effectively over much larger teams of programmers. Otherwise, the speed advantages of object-oriented programming will be sacrificed to the exponential overhead of human interaction as dozens or even hundreds of programmers attempt to understand the model and contribute to it.

The best way to avoid this exponential explosion of effort is to encapsulate the development of classes, as shown in Figure 8-8. Once the responsibilities of all classes are defined and documented, the actual development of these classes can be handed off to a cadre of dedicated class constructors.

There are several advantages to this strategy:

1. Only a small team of modelers has to understand the actual operation of the department. Class constructors need only understand the responsibilities of the individual classes they are to develop. This greatly reduces the amount of communication that has to take place among developers.

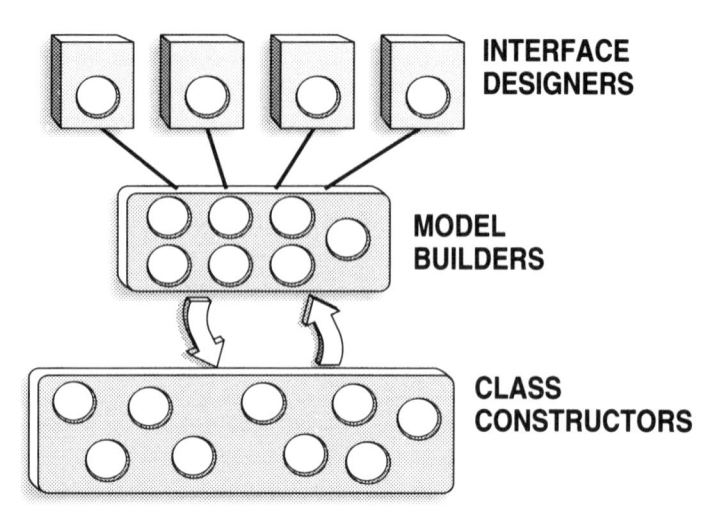

Figure 8-8: A New Division of Labor

2. Having class constructors build the classes "blind," with no knowledge of their context, provides an important test of the responsibility-based requirements analysis performed by the model builders. If a class constructor can't design and code a class from the requirements, the requirements are not well specified.

3. The resulting classes will tend to be more general-purpose than classes constructed to fit the needs of a particular model. This is a classic case of avoiding unintended bias. This increased generality enhances the reusability of the new classes in future development efforts.

We are now witnessing, and will continue to discuss, the demise of the monolithic application as illustrated in Figure 8-9.

As the classes are constructed, they should be designed to include a test capability. For example, if a personnel requisition class is constructed as part of the system, it should include the ability to test its expected behavior as it enters the system, when it is partially complete, when it is complete, and when it moves to the next processing step. This test bed includes the user interface into which the object fits: does it respond as expected to each message generated by the user, regardless of the state of the object?

ASSEMBLING THE CLASSES

Once the classes have been constructed, the modeling team assembles them and tests the behavior of the working model. This step consists of bringing

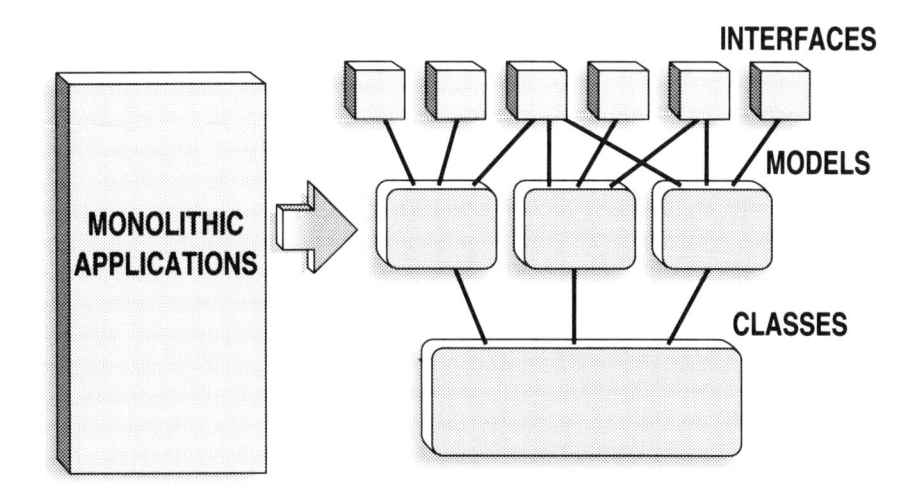

Figure 8-9: The Demise of the "Application"

together on a desktop the objects that must relate to or cooperate with one another and then testing their interfaces to be sure that expected behavior takes place.

For example, when the recruiter receives a personnel requisition, this object must be brought into contact with the database of job openings in the organization to be sure it finds appropriate matches.

CREATING ACTIVE OBJECTS

Having designed objects to be active in Step Three, we must now create those objects. Objects become active in one of three ways:

- menu scripts
- agent scripts
- methods within objects

Menu scripts are created entirely within COOPERATION. They should be used when all of the activity takes place within a single object and involves no interaction with other parts of the system.

Agent scripts, also created within COOPERATION, should be used when an activity involves multiple objects which must hand off assignments and information to other objects.

Methods, which are typically written in C++ when they are intended for use in COOPERATION objects, should be used only when the interaction involved is relatively stable, needs to be hidden from the end user, and is transparent.

DOCUMENT THE DESIGN
Don't forget to document the design and its implementation. Your plan should envision the creation of both written and electronic forms of documentation for users and for future designers who will need to understand your approach.

With COOPERATION's built-in Compound Document Editor and the hypertext-based help systems that Windows provides, you should consider providing more than the usual amount of on-line help for your users as well.

STEP SEVEN: DEPLOYMENT

With the classes and objects built, scripted, tested, and working together in the test-bed environment of the user interfaces, the time has come to deploy the departmental system. In most respects, deploying a COOPERATION system is not so different from deploying any other kind of system. It involves making the physical connections among workstations and server(s), parallel testing, installation on desktops, training and education, and on-going evaluation and optimization.

BEGIN WITH A SUB-SET OF THE DEPARTMENT
If possible, you should consider staging the system within the department by choosing a representative sub-set of the staff to set up initially. These people should represent each role in the organization. It may be necessary to set up a test area in or near the department to keep the disruption of physical network connections, placing new equipment on peoples' desks, and other such tasks from interrupting the department's work more than necessary.

It might prove difficult to try to run the department with part of its staff using COOPERATION and the rest doing things manually or using the old electronic system. Operating in parallel, as explained below, is probably essential to overcome this problem if it arises.

During this phase, you are likely to encounter some confusion about how tasks are to be accomplished, unforeseen conflicts between objects and their responsibilities, and other difficulties. You can iteratively fix these problems as they arise. This ability to test and fix iteratively in relatively com-pressed time frames is yet another benefit of using object-oriented programming and design.

OPERATE IN PARALLEL
After the initial problems have been identified and corrected and the system has run successfully in the sub-group, you should install the hardware and software through the rest of the department. This is the point where you are most likely to cause disruption. Scheduling the activity carefully, with department workload in mind and with good management support, can minimize the impact of this intrusion.

Once all of the department personnel have COOPERATION on their desks, it is a good idea if possible to run the system in parallel with the old system for at least one period. A period varies in length according to the department and its natural cycles. In an accounting group, it might be a month, while a personnel department might operate on weekly cycles.

TRAINING AND EDUCATION
Before and during installation and particularly during the first days of usage of the new system, users must be properly trained and educated. The difference between these two tasks is important.

All users must be trained in the techniques of using the system. Users with multiple roles must be educated so they understand the larger view and how their activities weave into the total COOPERATION system. They must also be re-educated in how they get their work done with the assistance of the new system.

EVALUATION
Once the system has been in place long enough for the users to become accustomed to it, you should re-visit the department and run tests to determine the new levels of the metrics you used during the analysis phase (Step Two).

This evaluation, along with interviews with users, should be used to determine if the design needs modification, if more tasks could be automated than first thought, and how users are reacting to the system. This information is invaluable as you deploy COOPERATION through the rest of the enterprise.

ON-GOING OPTIMIZATION
When you conduct evaluations, you may find things that can be fixed. These may involve problems in the design, places where the design didn't quite match up with the model or where the model didn't quite match up with reality. Or they may just be places you didn't originally envision could be enhanced by automation with COOPERATION.

Make these optimizing changes as appropriate and deploy them with the same care as the original system. And keep track of the kinds of things you encounter; you may be able to use this information to make the automation of other departments go more smoothly.

SOLVING BUSINESS PROBLEMS WITH COOPERATION

We've been digging around in the details of a COOPERATION design and deployment for quite a while now and it may have felt a bit strange to you, particularly if you have some previous systems analysis or design and programming experience. In case you're having trouble putting your finger on what's different, we thought we'd just lay it out for you.

We have just created a multi-user solution to a broad and important business problem without once thinking or talking in terms of a monolithic application. We didn't design and build a personnel requisition sub-system consisting of thousands of lines of traditional programming code. In this New Age of Software Components, we simply selected the right COOPERATION pieces to use and the right interfaces with which to stitch them together. We added a little mortar and perhaps wrote a few specialized methods. But we didn't build a program in the traditional sense.

Not only have we been able to build a comprehensive and useful system with only a fraction of the normal programming effort and expertise, we have used scripting languages and graphic interfaces to enable its users to make a broad range of modifications to the system without intervention by programmers.

It should be obvious to you that this was not a coincidence. COOPERATION itself is made up of numerous off-the-shelf applications "glued" together in a seamlessly integrated environment that supports the kind of problem-solving we've been doing in this chapter.

The Epilogue extends the experience of this chapter to the enterprise.

EPILOGUE

Transforming the Enterprise

COOPERATION can have a profound effect on the functioning of a single department, but its full advantages will not become apparent until it is applied to the organization as a whole. In fact, no one really knows what the full impact of such a system will be on a large organization. COOPERATION is the first object-based, integrated office system to support cooperative work on an enterprise scale. We believe that some highly empowering effects are possible at the enterprise level, but no company has yet taken the technology to this level. We are truly exploring unknown territory here.

However, several companies are now deploying COOPERATION in multiple departments, so we have a few lessons to pass on. What follows is our best attempt to help you make the transition to a larger scope of operation and gain the maximum leverage from COOPERATION-based corporate management.

A PLAN FOR CONTROLLED DEPLOYMENT

This section presents a plan for the controlled deployment of COOPERATION through the rest of the enterprise. This process has the following components:

- learning from the first departmental experiences as discussed in Chapter 8
- building on the success of the first department to evangelize the rest of the departments and prepare them for their involvement in the deployment
- devising a roll-out schedule
- creating the required inter-departmental tasks and applications
- expanding to encompass the entire enterprise

These steps are shown graphically in Figure 9-1.

LEARN FROM THE FIRST DEPARTMENT

The first step toward full deployment is to learn as much as possible from the first departmental application. As described in the first half of this chapter, careful measures should have been made of efficiency both before and after the installation of COOPERATION. More importantly, ratings of effectiveness should also have been taken to ensure that people are not

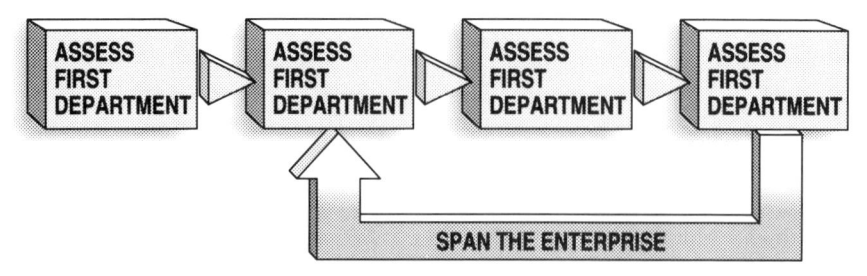

Figure 9-1: A Plan for Controlled Deployment

simply working faster but actually doing a better job. Given that these conclusions are true, the results should be studied to determine what techniques were most effective and which yielded the least gains. Of course, the effects of the ongoing optimization should be included in this analysis.

Candor is, of course, critical to this process. A great many information systems have failed because pressure from upper management to show positive results biased the reports on actual performance. To avoid this failing with COOPERATION, everyone should view the first department as a learning experience and critique it honestly to determine which techniques worked well and where improvements need to be made. The approach to deploying COOPERATION in the second department should be modified based on these findings, and the deployment in the third department should be refined further still. Moreover, these lessons should be applied back to the original departments both to enhance their functioning and to keep the functioning of all departments fully compatible.

CARRY THE MESSAGE TO THE MASSES

The deployment of a system like COOPERATION is usually a highly visible event throughout an organization even if the introduction takes place in only one department. People throughout the company will have heard rumors and second-hand reports of major changes going on, and they will naturally be curious about the system and concerned about its effects on their jobs. New computer systems can be intimidating to people at every level of the organization, and it's important to manage the spread of information about COOPERATION in a positive way.

The best way to do this is through a systematic program of education. Once you have successfully deployed COOPERATION in a single department, you should take that success story throughout the company. It is important to stress that COOPERATION is different from some of the "office automation" systems of the past, which often automated work to a point where staff were reduced to keyboarding automatons. With COOPERATION, the ability for people to bring their unique skills to the collective effort of the organization can actually be increased rather than reduced, allowing them to realize their potential more fully than was possible in the past. Properly presented, this can be an exciting prospect and a good motivating factor for cooperating with the deployment of the system.

Another important message is that, unlike other systems people may have used, the iconic interface of COOPERATION is intuitive and easy to operate. This is best communicated through live, big-screen demonstrations of the system in which the focus is on the enhancement of the work environment rather than the wizardry of the technology. For example, most people immediately grasp the idea of picking up folders and dropping them in mail baskets, and they quickly come to enjoy the physical manipulation of a virtual office environment.

We have also observed that COOPERATION users like the idea that they can have multiple desktops in COOPERATION and switch easily from task to task without having to clear their desks each time or deal with increasing clutter. Showing COOPERATION in this light and – facilities permitting – allowing people to play with the system can be a highly effective way of overcoming resistance to change.

Another strong motivating factor is testimonials from people who made the change and prefer their new mode of working. If possible, have individual members of the department talk informally about their experiences in making the transition and their feelings about the new work environment. Encourage them to be candid and interactive – a scripted, universally glowing testimonial can reduce credibility and may actually do more harm than good.

DETERMINE A ROLL-OUT SCHEDULE

As the education process continues, a plan should be prepared to determine the best roll-out sequence for deploying COOPERATION in other departments. Several considerations might apply to developing this sequence. One is to work with families of related departments. For example, if you started with Order Entry, you may want to do Shipping next because their close ties will increase the effectiveness of COOPERATION-based activities. This approach also lays the foundation for inter-department applications, which we discuss in the next section.

Another consideration is to focus on departments which are known bottlenecks in the overall corporate process. If inventory management is out of control and costing the company money in excess inventory, then that may be the next department to tackle regardless of how closely it's related to the pilot department.

A third consideration is risk management. Even if you had great success with the first department, you could still falter on the second. In general, it's a good idea to roll COOPERATION from peripheral activities toward the core of the organization rather than tackling the most central, mission critical departments first. Here's a case in point: Administration is a natural place to apply COOPERATION because it carries out so many routine tasks that keep the company flowing smoothly. But by the same token, if this department doesn't make the transition to COOPERATION in a graceful manner the aftershocks will be felt in every other department.

As you are sequencing departments for the roll out, be aware that some of the considerations that applied to the selecting the pilot department no longer apply to the remainder of the sequence. For example, you should no longer strive to avoid the problems of information integration and corporate politics. At this point, you should be ready to use COOPERATION to carry out information integration. And if turf wars are still going on, then you need to step up your management education program rather than trying to postpone the issue.

BUILD INTER-DEPARTMENT TASKS AND APPLICATIONS

As soon as you have COOPERATION running in two or more departments, you can begin to tie those departments together with inter-department tasks, scripts, objects, and applications. For example, a manufacturing company might deploy the system in engineering, then roll it out into manufacturing. Once these two departments were running under COOPERATION, it would be relatively easy to increase the cooperation between them. This cooperation, in turn, could result in better products, lower manufacturing costs, faster turn-around, or any combination of these competitive advantages.

Let's make this example more concrete. One of the major goals of contemporary manufacturing companies is *concurrent engineering*, an interaction between engineering and manufacturing that leads to products that are actually designed for manufacturability. The difficulty in implementing concurrent engineering is that each department is an "island of automation," using its own dedicated tools to facilitate its work independently of the needs of the other department. For example, engineering may use a CAD (computer-aided design) package to design parts, and manufacturing might use an MRP II (Manufacturing Resource Planning) system to manage production. These two systems would be completely independent—they would have no way of communicating with each other, nor would they speak a common language even if they could communicate.

As shown in Figure 9-2, COOPERATION provides a natural platform for implementing concurrent engineering. First, a design team should be established for each new product, and it should include the appropriate personnel from engineering, manufacturing, and—ideally—the QA department as well. All the relevant information about engineering, manufacturing and testing would be contained in a common set of folders which the team would share. This would ensure that everyone worked from the same information at all times. The team would then iterate on optimizing a design. Engineering would use its CAD tools to create an initial design and manufacturing would estimate the time and cost to produce the product according to that design. These results, together with suggestions for reducing costs, would go back to engineering, which would make changes to improve manufacturability. This iteration would continue until the team agreed that they had reached the best optimization available within their budgetary or time constraints.

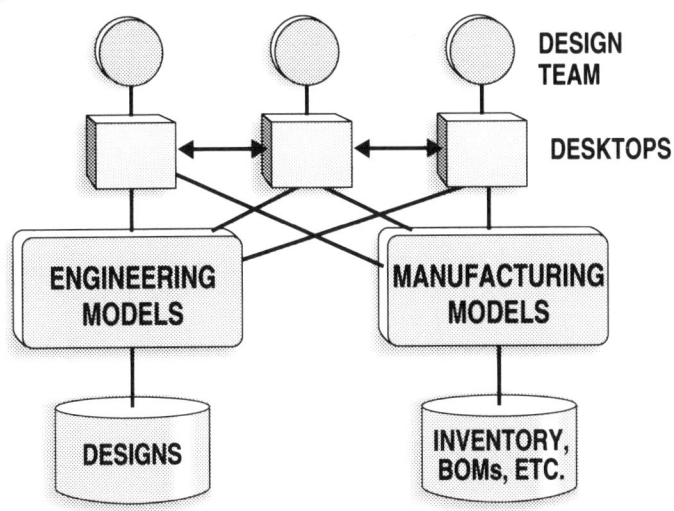

Figure 9-2: Concurrent Engineering through COOPERATION

All these interactions can take place through COOPERATION desktops, folders and agents. The system administrator would begin by setting up members of each team as groups with a shared set of folders and access to applications and other services. As the two groups cooperated together, they would gradually build up collections of compound documents that could, in turn, contain reports, diagrams, drawings, plans, spreadsheet forecasts and other objects. Using COOPERATION Mail, the group members could pass these objects around on the network without concern for where each individual object might be stored.

Each user would have a desktop that captured his or her role in the process. Many users might have multiple desktops so that they can easily and quickly switch roles in response to needs of the other group or of members of their own group.

System administrators could assist in the initial design of agent task scripts to establish the basic workflow automation. When an engineer made a modification to a drawing, the mere act of closing that document or its window could trigger an agent script that would see to it that all of the right manufacturing people received copies of the updated information via the mail system. Over time, users would learn how to modify these scripts and create their own to accommodate changing requirements and circumstances.

When face-to-face meetings were necessary – an occurrence which should become less frequent when cooperative tasks can be accomplished efficiently using the COOPERATION solution – one person can schedule the meeting, send out a notice over COOPERATION Mail to all attendees and identify the right conference room and other facilities, all with a few mouse clicks.

Engineering personnel could have Business Information Monitor objects on their desktops that would enable them to monitor inventory levels of a component they were about to change, and set thresholds for that value so they would disrupt manufacturing minimally when the change was ready. Such information would be very useful in prioritizing Engineering workload. If the inventory level was such that a BIM forecast indicated it would be several months before it would be low enough that a change would not be disruptive, the engineer responsible for that component might be able to shift his attention to a more critical task – or schedule a much-needed vacation – and know that the task could wait.

By now, you get the idea. We could go on with this scenario and keep bringing in more elements of COOPERATION in the process, but our purpose is not to design a complete COOPERATION-based concurrent engineering system. Rather, we want to give you some ideas for the breadth and depth of the activities COOPERATION can automate.

Notice that implementing concurrent engineering under COOPERATION does not require the development of new, monolithic applications. This is one of the key advantages of COOPERATION's open, object-based architecture. Local tasks such as design and manufacturing can be carried out using existing commercial packages. COOPERATION ties these packages together into a larger corporate environment that supports real-time interaction across the departments. This approach to concurrent engineering is far less expensive than developing a monolithic application, it leverages the company's existing investment in design and manufacturing systems, and it provides a level of flexibility that no hard-coded application could ever provide.

SPAN THE ENTERPRISE

COOPERATION was intended from its inception to be a tool for integrating the entire enterprise. Stopping short of this goal can yield benefits, but there are much greater benefits to be gained by getting everyone up and running under the same management system. By spanning the entire organization, you ensure that everyone has simultaneous, controlled access to the same corporate information, and you facilitate communication and cooperation at every level of the company. In fact, once you reach this point you may find your company beginning to change in some fundamental ways.

For example, it is a natural extension of concurrent engineering to move toward a full computer-integrated manufacturing (CIM) environment, which is currently the "holy grail" among manufacturers. Instead of simply linking engineering and manufacturing together, a product team would include people in marketing, sales, quality assurance, distribution, finance, and all the other departments that are involved in the creation and release of a new product. All would share access to the same base of information about a product, tapping the aspects they need and contributing according to their needs and expertise. If production costs began to encroach on anticipated profits, finance could raise a red flag and cause engineering and manufacturing to focus on reducing costs. Alternatively, if cost-reduction measures began to eliminate features that were essential to the success of the product, marketing could step in and set the product back on course. Because all of these interactions were taking place electronically rather than through memos and meetings, the feedback would be very fast and corrective actions could be far more effective and economical than engineering changes made at a later date.

It is easy to imagine similar transformations in service companies. For example, an insurance company could assemble a team to develop and deliver a new combination policy. This team would include people from marketing, sales, underwriting, accounting, legal, and other departments to ensure that the new package was a good balance among the needs of the varying constituencies of these departments, as shown in Figure 9-3.

Again, no new monolithic applications are required to bring about this kind of enterprise integration. COOPERATION provides all the necessary tools to form the teams, share the information, automate the administrative aspects, and speed the new package to market.

ENHANCING CORPORATE COMMUNICATIONS

One of the most interesting and pleasant side effects of a COOPERATION installation is the degree to which communications within the enterprise can be enhanced. The speed and band-width of communications can be increased, and remote communications between far-flung parts of the enterprise can be facilitated in ways that are simply not possible without advanced technology.

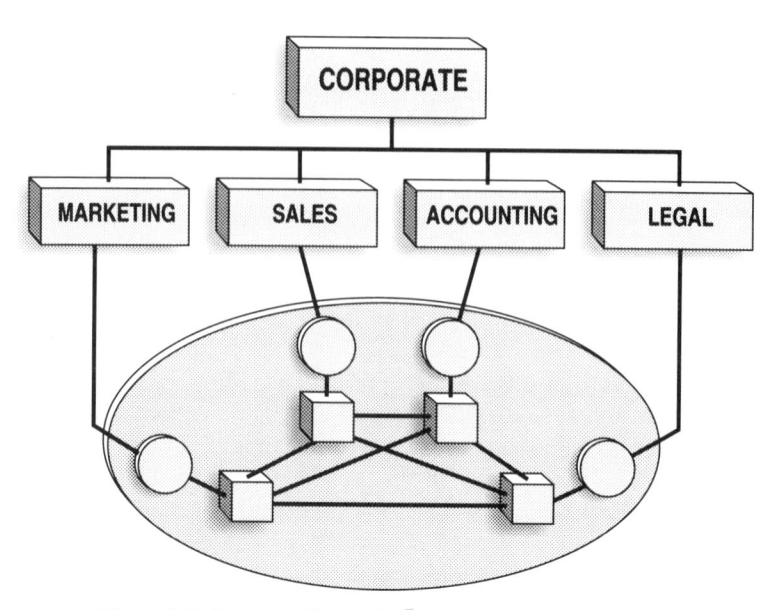

Figure 9-3: Dynamic Formation of COOPERATION Terms

INCREASING THE SPEED AND BANDWIDTH OF COMMUNICATIONS

COOPERATION can increase the speed of communications dramatically. Where it once took a day or two to get a memo out to your fellow managers, or perhaps a week to set up an important meeting, you can now interact electronically and reach decisions in a matter of minutes or hours. Multiplied across the organization, this acceleration of communication can greatly increase management effectiveness. In a business environment in which a few hours can make the difference between a huge profit and a devastating loss, the glacial pace of memo-based communications is a luxury that organizations can no longer afford.

Not only can COOPERATION increase the speed of communications among managers and workers, it can also increase the amount of information that is communicated in any given message. Instead of a simple memo, which carries only a small amount of text-based information, managers can just as easily send complete folders containing documents, images, charts, and other multimedia information. Moreover, since there are no duplication costs, this complete package of information can be distributed simultaneously to an entire team, allowing all members of the team to respond to a situation with all the relevant information in front of them on their screens.

IMPLEMENTING REMOTE, ASYNCHRONOUS COMMUNICATIONS

As organizations move increasingly into the global arena, effective communications between remote sites becomes critical to the successful coordination of efforts. Because it hides the communication channel below the level of personal interactions, COOPERATION makes no distinction between local and remote communications. Teams distributed across three continents could interact almost as quickly and easily as teams based in the same building.

Of course, teams distributed over multiple continents will necessarily be operating in different time zones. This separation in time as well as space renders traditional forms of synchronous communications, such as meetings or telephone conversations, impractical as the primary mode of interaction. By contrast, electronic communications need not be synchronous and, in fact, more often take place asynchronously.

For example, a team member in Brazil may post a folder containing the results of a new market survey as soon as the results are available, without waiting to convene a meeting or even considering bringing people together in the same room. This folder would quickly appear on all the team members desks, regardless of their locations, and each could react electronically as soon as it was convenient, depending on other demands on their time as well as differences in local time.

EXPANDING THE SCOPE OF THE ENTERPRISE

Traditionally, an enterprise has been viewed as a group of people banded together to conduct a business. Specifically, the enterprise consisted of the employees, equipment, and other tangible assets of an organization, together with certain intangibles such as good will. In recent years, however, there has been a trend toward viewing the enterprise in a much larger scope, one which includes many elements once regarded as the "environment" of the company. This expanded view of the enterprise is depicted graphically in Figure 9-4.

BRINGING CUSTOMERS INTO YOUR BUSINESS

The best example of this is "customers." Customers are obviously essential to a business, but they are somehow viewed as being down at the end of the line, the distant consumers of the organizational output.

There has been a strong movement over the last ten years to make customers the focal point of business operations. This is such an obviously correct idea that it's sometimes hard to imagine how so many books get published (and purchased!) which do nothing more than espouse this idea. What is usually missing in these books is a good mechanism for actually bringing customers' needs to the constant attention of everyone in the company who can contribute to meeting those needs.

COOPERATION can provide such a mechanism. Where customers are themselves organizations, they can easily be equipped with real-time

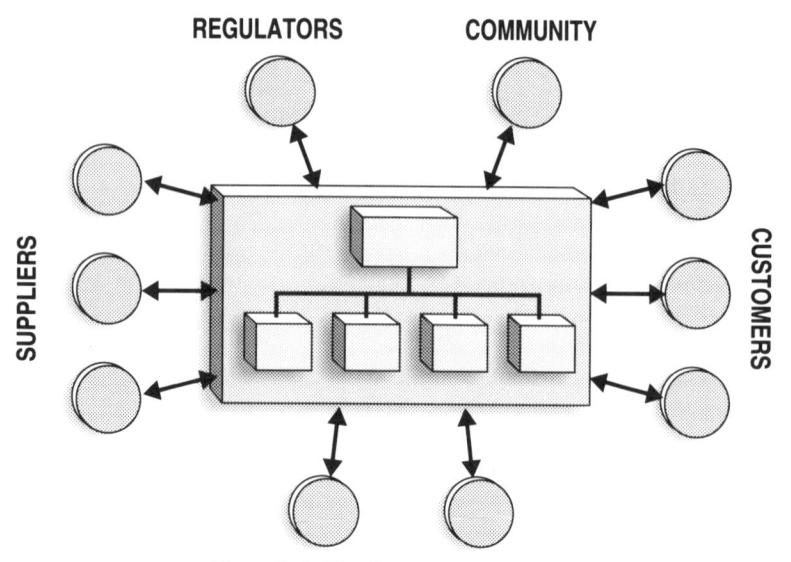

Figure 9-4: The Scope of the Enterprise

connections to an organization through COOPERATION desktops. Of course, their access privileges would be restricted and their roles would differ from those of employees, but they could nonetheless become an integral part of the organization. For example, customers could "sit in" electronically on design reviews, making suggestions for improvements while products are still in the planning stage. They could also provide real-time feedback on product quality, pricing, and other decisions which affect them, helping a company respond to their concerns quickly.

This increased responsiveness to customer needs would help companies avoid poorly targeted products, track changing requirements in a timely manner, and enhance customer loyalty. Companies which include their customers in their internal affairs may initially experience some nervousness about letting "outsiders" into their private chambers, and they may suffer a few embarrassing revelations as customers discover how the business really works. But they will ultimately profit from their openness and will enjoy a considerable competitive edge against companies which remain closed to their customers.

BETTER SERVICE THROUGH CLOSER TIES TO VENDORS

On the other side of the business, vendors can also be equipped with COOPERATION facilities to allow closer ties and better fulfillment of needs. This tightened linkage is so productive that it is now absolutely essential to modern manufacturing. For example, General Motors' master production schedule was once a closely guarded secret. Now it is electronically broadcast to all its major vendors and automatically incorporated into their own production schedules so that they respond as quickly as possible to GM's constantly changing requirements.

To cite an even tighter relationship, Japanese manufacturers are so closely linked to their vendors that they actually control many aspects of production, quality, and pricing, often on a real-time basis. These vendors may, in turn, be tightly linked to their own vendors, creating an ongoing symphony of synchronized operations in which it is increasingly difficult to draw sharp distinctions as to where one "enterprise" leaves off and another begins.

MAINTAINING CONTACT WITH THE OUTSIDE WORLD
Corporations are also affected by the events of the world around them, from commodity price fluctuations to outbreaks of hostility in foreign lands. Increasingly, modern organizations are automating the collection of relevant information over newswire services and other information providers and incorporating what they learn into their moment-to-moment decisions.

In fact, one early adopter of COOPERATION, a major financial institution, has made the collection and distribution of outside information an essential part of its electronic management system, automatically keeping all of its managers advised of relevant changes in the external environment. This company will undoubtedly enjoy a significant competitive advantage over financial companies which rely on newspapers or radio reports to track events that affect their decisions.

COPING WITH SUSTAINED CHANGE

The days when a company could devise an operating plan, organize for that plan, and then settle down to efficient execution are long gone. The successful corporation today must be organized for constant change. Unlike conventional information systems, which often lock a company into a fixed mode of operation, COOPERATION uses the flexibility of object technology to help a company withstand and, where possible, even control change. In fact, COOPERATION's major contribution to managing change is to remove the technological obstacles. If management is willing and able to embrace change, COOPERATION can support the constant refinement required by today's ever-changing market.

Index

A
acceleration, 3
Action menu, 31
agent, 32
Agent Task Language, 5, 17, 34, 39, 42, 43, 105
agent tasks, xx, 34
    scheduling, 36
alarm status,
    BIM, 65
Ami Pro, 67
anthropomorphism, 102
API, *see Application Programming Interface*
application, 15
    integration, 17
    layer, 5
Application Programming Interface, 14, 74
Asymetrix ToolBook, 40
ATL, *see Agent Task Language*

B
BIM, *see Business Information Monitor*
bridges, 73
Business Information Monitor, 17, 20, 64, 104
business modeling, xxi

C
C++, 75, 109
calendar,
    group, 5, 17, 61
    individual, 5
    master, 18, 32, 62
    resource, 18, 64

CAT, *see Communications Authoring Tool*
change, xv, 3, 123
class, xii
class constructors, 107
collection, xviii
Communications Authoring Tool, 68, 71
complexity,
    managing, 4, 11
composite objects, xvii
compound document, xxii, 5, 21, 27, 67
    mailing, 19
compound document editor, 17, 19, 110
configuration, 87
container objects, xix
COOPERATION
    goals, 9
    implementing, 53
customization, 3

D
data, xiii
    ATL, 44
    types, 44
databases, 6, 20, 23, 77
DB2, 21, 79
DDE, 66
decentralization, 3
department
    choosing 94
design, 91
desktop, viii, xxii, 4, 27, 29, 31, 104
    agents, 34
    multiple, 4, 16, 29, 115

Disposition Category Profile, 84
Disposition Shelf Profile, 84
document, 77
    conversion, 84
    management, 23, 81
    profiles, 83
    storage, 6
Document Services, 77
DOS, 5, 12, 32, 61, 73, 86
dynamic binding, ix

E

Edit menu, 31
electronic mail, xix, 5, 17, 68
encapsulation, xiii, 97
end-user programming, 4, 39
enterprise, vii
Express Edit, 78

F

File Category Profiles, 83
file drawer, 32
files, xxii
folder, xix, 27, 105

G

globalization, 3
graphical user interface, 10, 12
group calendar, 5, 17, 61
GUI, *see graphical user interface*

H

hardware required, 57
Help menu, 31

Hewlett-Packard, 15
hierarchies, xv

I

icons, 15, 27, 115
Industrial Revolution, x
information hiding, xv
Information Services, 23, 77
Information Storage Manager, 23, 25, 80
inheritance, xv, xvi
installation, 55, 87
instance, xii
integration, 26, 72, 74
Interface Builder, 45
Inventive User, 40
ISM, *see Information Storage Manager*

J

job titles, 102

L

legacy, 15
    applications, 72
    software, 5
    systems, 57
links, 67

M

mail, 19, 24
Master Calendar, 18, 32, 62
masters, 29

menus
  action menu, 31
  edit menu, 31
  help menu, 31
  objects menu, 31
  settings menu, 31
  task menu, 31
  view menu, 31
messages, ix, xx
methodology
  deployment, 6, 91
  scripting, 46
methods, xiii
Microsoft Windows, 15
mini-applications, 42, 44
modularity, 3
multiple desktops, 4, 16, 29, 115

N

Network Print View tool, 85
NewWave, 15, 26, 74

O

Object Management Facility, xxii, 34
object technology, ix, xxi
Object-oriented programming, 39
objects, vii, x, 30
  creating, 28
  nature, xvi
  sharing, 33
Objects menu, 31, 74
OMF, *see Object Management Facility*
OPIs, 74

Oracle, 79
OS/2, 12

P

parameters, xx
password, 26, 89
polymorphism, ix
printers, 32, 84
printing, 6
procedures, xiii
programming
  vs. scripting, 40, 42

R

RAA, *see Remote Application Access*
Remote Application Access, 17, 68, 70
Remote Application Access Manager, 22
Report Windows, 78
resource calendar, 18, 64
responsibility-driven design, 101
reusability, ix, xii, 48
roles, 4, 16, 56, 94, 101, 102

S

scripting, viii, 4, 39, 43
scripts, 71
security, 25, 80, 82, 88, 89
  user environment, 25
server, 57
services layer, 5, 14, 22, 77
Settings menu, 31
Shelf Profile, 84

127

site licensing, 85
site preparation, 56
Smalltalk, 75
software installation, *see supply cabinet*
Software Supply Service, 77
Spinnaker PLUS, 40
spreadsheets, 20
SQL, 17, 21, 66
SQL*Net, 78
SQLBase, 22, 78
SQLTalk/Windows, 78
supply cabinet, 6, 25, 77, 86
System Management Services, 86

T

Task menu, 31
tasks
    creating, 35
    performing, 35
Text Retrieval engine, 23
text translation, 24
TIFF, 67

tools, 27, 31
training, 56, 92, 111, 114

U

UNIX, 12
User Profile, 87

V

version control, 80, 82
Version profiles, 83
view
    BIM, 65
View menu, 31

W

waste basket, 32
Windows, 26, 61, 66, 72, 74, 86, 110
word processors, 24
workflow, 96